Vintage Views of the Mackinac Straits Region

Martin–
Happy 80th Birthday–
Enjoy!

m. christine byron & Thomas R. Wilson

M. Christine Byron & Thomas R. Wilson

Foreword by Governor William G. Milliken

Arbutus Press • Traverse City, Michigan

Vintage Views of the Mackinac Straits Region © M. Christine Byron & Thomas R. Wilson 2007

Arbutus Press
Traverse City, Michigan
info@arbutuspress.com
www.Arbutuspress.com

ISBN 978-1-933926-10-0

Front cover photo: Courtesy of Teysen Photography, Mackinaw City, Michigan
Back cover photo: Courtesy of Archives of Michigan, hand-colored by Dianne Carroll Burdick, Grand Rapids, Michigan

Printed in Canada

First Edition

Library of Congress Cataloging-in-Publication Data available

Dedication

To all those travelers that over the years have visited this magical land. To their warm smiles in old photographs pasted in dusty scrapbooks. To their "wish you were here" messages sent on thousands of postcards to all parts of the country. To the souvenirs they brought home with memories of an unforgettable vacation.

Contents

Preface

Our love of Michigan and our fascination with its early tourist industry have poured out onto the pages of our books. This is the third book in our Vintage Views series. Our first book, *Vintage Views of Leelanau County,* was published in 2002. Our vacations in Leelanau and our interest in its history evolved into a wider interest in the history of tourism in the state of Michigan. *Vintage Views of the Charlevoix–Petoskey Region,* our second book, was published in 2005 and drew on the rich history of that old resort region. We then decided to turn our attention to that unique section of Michigan, the Straits region, with its long history and many scenic attractions. We have focused on Mackinaw City, St. Ignace and Mackinac Island. Of course, no history of the region would be complete without the story of the car ferries and the building of the Mackinac Bridge.

This book is intended to offer an overview of the history of the Straits region, with an emphasis on tourism and vacationing. We wanted to give a glimpse of vacation life from the 1860s to the 1960s. It was not our intention to delve deeply into the early history of the region. There are many good histories already written that cover this interesting topic. We also have not made an attempt to detail the construction of the Mackinac Bridge. We would refer the reader to more thorough resources on that subject cited in our bibliography. Our interest in the Mackinac Bridge was related to its impact on tourism in the region.

We hoped to take the reader back to the time of early travel and vacationing in the region. We have researched how the Mackinac Straits region was portrayed to the potential tourist and quoted from early travel brochures, newspapers, books and other sources. These early promotional materials often described tourist destinations in both exaggerated and flowery language that we find charming today. These promotional pieces and travel guides were often the reader's first exposure to the region. We also have used messages from the backs of postcards, inviting the reader to share someone else's vacation, from some other time and place.

We have used quotations from these historical sources to accompany vintage photographs, postcards, maps, advertisements, and other ephemera to capture the spirit of those early days. We have tried to pair quotations and images from the same time period. In quoting from these writings we have kept the original inaccuracies, misspellings, the incorrect grammar, and the sometimes politically incorrect language of the time. We have attempted to give a flavor of the past, without trying to document it in a dry, scholarly manner. We wanted to show what drew early travelers to the region and what vacationing was like in earlier times. We realize there may be gaps and omissions in our coverage of the Straits region. There were times that we could not locate an image or original quotation that suited our purpose.

It should be noted that names and spellings of various places changed over the years; we tried to use the most common variations. Names of ethnic groups also have variations. Although the term *American Indian* was used more commonly than *Native American*, we have chosen the latter because of its preferred usage.

We have drawn extensively from our personal collection of postcards and old tourist and travel ephemera, as well as using material gathered from archives, libraries and private collectors. We have acknowledged the sources of the images used in the credits at the end of the book.

We invite you to travel with us through the pages of *Vintage Views of the Mackinac Straits Region.* We have enjoyed the journey ourselves and hope you will too. To paraphrase an old tourist brochure from the area: No trip to Michigan is complete without visiting the famous Mackinac Straits region, a land of history and legend and spectacular beauty.

M. Christine Byron & Thomas R. Wilson

Acknowledgements

TOURIST CONVENTION, STATE PARK, MACKINAW CITY, MICH.   5A-H2419

Our thanks go out to those writers of the past 150 years who have written so eloquently on the Mackinac Straits region. We have used their words with all their flowery language and exaggeration to give a feel for life in bygone days.

For the generous gift of their time, knowledge and resources we extend special thanks to the various libraries, archives and museums we visited in the course of our research. In particular we acknowledge Julie Meyerle at the Archives of Michigan, Michigan Historical Center, Karen Jania at the Bentley Historical Library, University of Michigan, Carol Fink at the Library of Michigan, and Michelle Hewitt at the Boyne City Historical Museum. We also thank the professionals at the Clarke Historical Library, Central Michigan University, the Grand Rapids Public Library and the Mackinac State Historic Parks.

For use of historical promotional materials we express our gratitude to the Mackinaw City Chamber of Commerce, the St. Ignace Chamber of Commerce, and the West Michigan Tourist Association. For their helpful assistance, we also thank the Mackinac Island Tourism Bureau, the St. Ignace Visitors Bureau and the Mackinac Bridge Authority.

Our sincere gratitude goes to William J. Davis of G-I Holdings, Inc. for use of postcards from the L.L. Cook Company. Debra Gust from the Curt Teich Postcard Archives of the Lake County, Illinois Discovery Museum was most helpful. We also thank Dan Penrod from Penrod-Hiawatha for use of its published postcards. Jack Deo of Superior View was most kind in letting us use photographs from his collection, as was Thomas Pfeiffelmann of the Star Line Mackinac Island Hydro-Jet Ferry.

We extend our deepest thanks to the members of the Don Geske family for hanging on to those ephemeral pieces from their visits to the Mackinac region, and sharing their private collection with us. We also thank Alan Bennett for sharing his collection of Mackinac Island postcards.

For use of his wonderful photograph on our book's cover, we extend heartfelt thanks to Ken Teysen and Greg Teysen of Teysen Photography in Mackinaw City and Wooden Gallery in Traverse City. We also thank the Archives of Michigan for use of the back cover photo, which was exquisitely hand-colored by Dianne Carroll Burdick.

Marcie Beck read the manuscript and pointed out many areas for improvement. We are deeply indebted to her for her guidance, patience, perseverance and skill with the English language. Julie Christianson Stivers was also most helpful with editorial guidance.

Rebecca Near did a fantastic job scanning many of the images used in the book. Her expertise guided us over many a bumpy road. We couldn't have done it without her.

There have been many other people who were greatly supportive, each in his or her own way. We thank Richard Vettese, Karolee Hazlewood, Carl Bajema, LeRoy Barnett, Dan Konkle and George Weeks for their assistance, encouragement and advice.

And for making our dream a reality, special thanks from the bottom of our hearts, goes to Susan Bays, our publisher, dear friend and guidance counselor.

Foreword

The Straits of Mackinac have been the crossroads of the Great Lakes since the first inhabitants came to the region. What better way to look at this vitally important area of Michigan than through the lens of travel and tourism? Christine Byron and Tom Wilson have created a thoughtful, entertaining, and visually stunning book that honors the unique history, scenic beauty, and entrepreneurial spirit of the Straits area.

Michigan's wonderful Straits of Mackinac is rich in history, commerce, natural resources and recreational opportunities. Native Americans celebrated the area as a sacred refuge and place of abundance, 17th century explorers and fur traders found ample riches, Victorian vacationers streamed north by boat and rail for delightful summers, and hundreds of thousands of automobile travelers brought new economic opportunities to the region, first by way of ferries, more recently by crossing the mighty Mackinac Bridge.

"There is a charm that lingers long in the memory of the view across the water of the Straits," says a 1915 guide to the West Michigan Pike, quoted in this book. "Here do you exclaim, with thousands who have preceded you: 'In All the World, No Trip Like This'." Linger long with this remarkable book, and discover one of the world's great places, Michigan's Straits of Mackinac.

William G. Milliken

Lone Birch, Mackinac Island, Mich.   Published by C.H. Wickman

The reconstructed stockade of Fort Michilimackinac in Mackinaw City stands in contrast to the modern marvel of the Mackinac Bridge. The opening of the Bridge in 1957 marked a momentous point in the history of the Straits region.

Chapter One – The Straits Region

The blue-green waters of the Straits of Mackinac wed Lake Michigan and Lake Huron and separate the Upper and Lower Peninsulas. The Straits are 26 miles wide at the eastern or Lake Huron entrance, and 13 miles wide at the Lake Michigan side. The narrowest part is 4.5 miles wide where it is spanned by the Mackinac Bridge. Thousands of freighters and pleasure boats pass through the Straits annually. The islands in the Straits include Mackinac and Bois Blanc, both inhabited, and Round and St. Helena, smaller and uninhabited. The cities of the Straits region are Mackinaw City at the "tip of the mitt" in the Lower Peninsula and St. Ignace at the southern point of the Eastern Upper Peninsula.

The Straits of Mackinac are regarded as the "Crossroads of the Great Lakes." The Straits were the route between Lake Huron and Lake Michigan for Native Americans, explorers, adventurers, fur traders and missionaries. From the 17th century into the 19th century, the French, British and Native Americans fought for control of this strategic spot and the lucrative fur trade that passed through it. After being under the flags of France and Britain, the area finally came under the secure possession of the United States in 1815.

Native Americans were the earliest inhabitants in the region. It is estimated that as many as 7,000 Ottawa (Odawa) and Chippewa (Ojibway) Indians were spending part of the year at the Straits when the first of the fur traders came. The Native Americans hunted and fished the area. They had a great reverence for Mackinac Island and the history of the Island abounds with Native American legends.

In 1634 Jean Nicolet, the French explorer, was the first European to pass through the Straits. He was followed by other European explorers and adventurers who came throughout the 1600s. The first to settle in the region were the French fur traders who came to the area known as Michilimackinac in canoes from scattered trading posts with their collection of furs to be sold. Furs for fashionable hats and coats were in great demand in Europe. The French called the Straits region Michilimackinac, an Indian word meaning "the Land of the Great Turtle." The term was sometimes used interchangeably with Mackinac Island.

Jesuit missionaries followed in the footsteps of the fur traders. Father Jacques Marquette established a mission at St. Ignace in 1671. Other missionaries also settled in the area with hopes of converting the Native Americans to Christianity. Many of the French explorers and missionaries left a legacy in Michigan place names including Father Jacques Marquette, Antoine de la Mothe Cadillac and Pierre Francois Xavier de Charlevoix.

The area was rife with wars, massacres and rivalry for the wealth of the fur trade. Forts were established at Michilimackinac and Mackinac Island and played roles in the French and Indian War and the War of 1812. In 1783 under the Treaty of Paris, Michilimackinac became part of the United States Territory, but it was occupied by British troops until 1796 when American troops finally took possession. During the War of 1812 the British recaptured Fort Mackinac. The Treaty of Ghent ended that war in 1815 and gave the fort back to the Americans. America now had a monopoly on the fur trade and John Jacob Astor centered his American Fur Trading Company business on Mackinac Island. It thrived for several decades until the sharp decline in the fur trade forced closure of the Company in 1842.

Thousands of early immigrants passed through the Straits on their journey farther west. The next wave of travelers were vacationers who came to Mackinac Island, a new resort that was becoming popular in the 1870s. Water was the main avenue of travel for decades and several steamship companies made Mackinac Island one of their ports-of-call.

The first railroad to reach Mackinaw City was the Michigan Central in 1881. The Grand Rapids & Indiana Railway followed in 1882. The Detroit & Mackinac Railway reached Cheboygan in 1904, but never managed to complete its run to Mackinaw City. The three railroads brought thousands of vacationers from the Lower Peninsula to the Straits every summer. In the Upper Peninsula the Detroit, Mackinac & Marquette Railway brought passengers and freight from Duluth to St. Ignace in 1881. By 1886 the line had evolved into the Duluth, South Shore & Atlantic Railroad. In the days before the State took over ferry service, railroad car ferries would take motorists and vehicles across the Straits.

The popularity of the automobile and the development of good roads slowly changed the way most of these vacationers arrived at the Straits. Roadside services sprang up in Mackinaw City and St. Ignace to meet the needs of the motoring public. The highlight of many trips to the region was a visit to Mackinac Island. When the Mackinac Bridge opened in 1957, it became a national tourist attraction. As a new century begins, the scenic beauty and rich history of the Straits region continue to draw visitors, adventurers and entrepreneurs.

Lovely Waters of the Straits of Mackinac

"Particularly lovely among all the lovely waters of Michigan are the Straits of Mackinac. They join Lake Huron and Lake Michigan. They separate the Upper Peninsula from the Lower Peninsula. Three islands narrow the opening – gem-like Mackinac Island, wooded Bois Blanc, and tiny Round Island.

Freighters bound between Lake Michigan and southern Lake Huron take the South Channel between Bois Blanc and the Southern Peninsula mainland; passenger boats and freighters bound between Lake Michigan and Lake Superior take the main channel between Mackinac Island and Round Island. All pass between Mackinaw City and the St. Ignace peninsula, which projects down from the Upper Peninsula, with northern Lake Huron on one side of it and Lake Michigan on the other."

-Arthur Stace, *Touring the Coasts of Michigan*, 1937-1938

Map Straits of Mackinac.

Bird's Eye View of the famous Mackinac Region, showing the Water Routes to Petoskey, Sault Ste. Marie and Lake Superior, and the D., M. & M. R. R. to Marquette and Lake Superior. Good Fishing and Hunting.

Postcard message:

August 26

Dear Folks:
So far, so good. Just landed about 15 minutes ago. Had a lower
berth and a good sleep and breakfast – but doubt if I can get a berth
to Detroit –such a crowd. But a beautiful place. Am going to look for
some "eats" now.

-Love, Mildred

Postmarked Mackinac Island 1909
Mailed to Escanaba, Mich.

10019. THE DOCK AND MISSION POINT. MACKINAC ISLAND. MICH.

Panorama of Ships

"All the shipping of the Upper Lakes passes through the Mackinac Straits, and the visitor beholds an unceasing panorama by day and night of the commerce of the inland seas. There is a charm that lingers long in the memory of the view across the water of the Straits, and of the islands which dot them. Round Island and Bois Blanc, to the southeast; Les Cheneaux Islands, famous for their fishing, to the northeast; St. Ignace, at the southern extremity of the Upper Peninsula, to the northwest: Mackinaw City to the southwest…

All passenger lines that ply the Great Lakes stop at Mackinac Island. Ferry connection at Mackinaw City, 6 miles distant, with the Grand Rapids & Indiana and Michigan Central Railroads… Here do you exclaim, with thousands who have preceded you; 'In All the World, No Trip Like This'."

-West Michigan Pike Assoc., *Maps, Routes and Tourist Directory of the West Michigan Pike*, 1915

8851 STR. 'NORTH LAND' AT THE DOCK, MACKINAC ISLAND, MICH.

Postcard message:

July 29, 1907

Dear Richard,
After 3 days/2 nights of lake ride we arrived here. It is a
beauty spot. Wish you were here. We're right on the lake-
front. Trust you are all well. Remember me to all.

-With love, Ella

Postmarked Mackinac Island. 1907
Mailed to Richmond, Ind.

Steamship Lines

Steamship lines began regular passenger service to the Straits in the 1870s. As tourism developed, more and more ships made Mackinac Island and St. Ignace ports-of-call. Advertisers claimed travel by boat was less expensive than rail, and avoided the dust and discomforts of train travel. Some of the larger ships were "floating palaces" and offered sophisticated amenities including elegant saloons, first-class dining facilities, dance orchestras and comfortable staterooms. The "changing scenery and fresh, bracing air" were touted as health benefits of travel by water. Travel by steamship peaked about 1900 and continued to fare quite well over the next twenty or thirty years when Great Lakes cruises were popular. With the rising popularity of the automobile and the economic effects of the Depression, the steamship lines gradually lost ground in the 1930s. Over the years there were many companies whose ships serviced the Straits. Some of these were the Detroit & Cleveland Navigation Company, the Goodrich Transportation Company, the Michigan Transit Corp., the Chicago, Duluth & Georgian Bay Line, the Northern Steamship Line, the Great Lakes Transit Company, the Northern Navigation Company and the Owen Sound Transportation Company. The Georgian Bay Line ran the last of the Great Lakes cruises to the Straits. The company offered the leisurely trips on the *S.S. North American* and the *S.S. South American* until the 1960s.

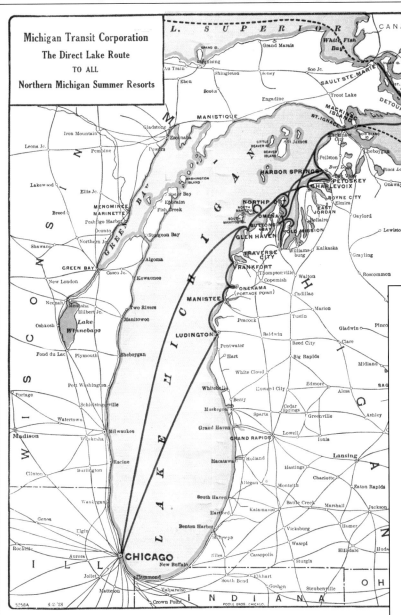

Michigan Transit Corporation
The Direct Lake Route
TO ALL
Northern Michigan Summer Resorts

"**Mackinac Island Cruises** – Departures from Chicago every Monday and Friday (except July 4th) during the summer season. More than a 24-hour stop-over is allowed at Mackinac Island on the Monday sailings, July 14th to August 31st. Fares: $17.00 One Way, $33.00 Round Trip, Meals and Berth included. A radical reduction under fares in effect last season. Only lake line to Mackinac offering stops en route at charming resorts in Northern Michigan."

-Michigan Transit Corp., *Vacation Lake Trips*, 1930

SEASON 1928

Michigan Transit Corporation

S. S. MANITOU at Mackinac Island—"Fairy Isle of the Northland"

VACATION LAKE CRUISES AND DIRECT STEAMSHIP SERVICE BETWEEN CHICAGO AND ALL NORTHERN MICHIGAN SUMMER RESORTS

The MICHIGAN TRANSIT CORPORATION, **with five sailings every week from Chicago on summer schedule,** serves practically all northern West Michigan summer resorts from Ludington to Mackinac Island, inclusive, and Sault Ste. Marie, with an unusually efficient and popular direct steamship service, including Vacation Cruises—"Just Long Enough," at popular prices.

Everyone, young and old, needs a vacation each summer, and that vacation should be just as different from one's daily routine of life as it is possible to make it. For real comfort and thorough enjoyment there is no substitute for summer travel on the popular lake liners "Manitou" and "Puritan" between Chicago and northern West Michigan Summer Resorts. An investment in health that pays big dividends.

STEAMSHIPS "MANITOU" and "PURITAN" are large, modern, commodious steel passenger steamers of exceptional tonnage. Both well and favorably known from Coast to Coast for their steadiness, cleanliness and accommodations for the guests' comfort and safety. Dining rooms located in the main cabin forward, and are inviting and well ventilated. Fish dinners a specialty. Employees of the Michigan Transit Corporation are chosen for their efficiency and for their desire to extend to all passenger-guests willing, cheerful and courteous service. Suggestions for the betterment of service always welcome. Modern radio equipment aboard ship keeps passengers in touch with shore stations at all times. Wide, unobstructed promenade decks afford opportunities to bask in the sunshine and enjoy the everchanging panorama of wonderful scenery or brisk walks for exercise. The cool, crisp water-washed air is a real tonic for tired nerves.

Georgian Bay Liners
S.S. North American and *S.S. South American*
Sister Queens of the Great Lakes

"Free from gasoline fumes and the cares of driving, today's happy vacationers retrace the paths of voyageurs from olden times as they sail on one of the adventure-packed cruises of the 'Queens of the Great Lakes' – the *S.S. North American* and *S.S. South American*.

From May to September these great ships sail the Great Lakes, giving delightful days of cruising to such famous and historic points as Mackinac Island, 'Bermuda of the North'… Both the *North* and her sister ship the *South* are modern and comfortable in every respect. The only ships on the Great Lakes designed and built exclusively for cruising, they carry only passengers, with every well-appointed room an OUTSIDE room. There are top side sun, sports and observation decks, a sheltered and carpeted promenade deck completely encircling the ships, radar and ship to shore telephone service, and there is no smoke or soot from these oil fueled floating palaces to take the sparkle from the brilliant lake air.

Both *North* and *South* make stopovers at all important points along the thrill-packed cruise—you can enjoy a carriage ride at Mackinac Island or a thrilling side trip to Niagara Falls. Both one way and round trip passage can be arranged between cruise ports."

-Mackinac Island: The Magazine Guide, circa 1940

DETROIT & CLEVELAND NAVIGATION CO.

D&C

LAKE LINES
DETROIT - CLEVELAND
BUFFALO - NIAGARA FALLS
MACKINAC ISLAND
ST. IGNACE
CHICAGO

THE GRAND FLEET OF THE GREAT LAKES

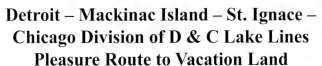

Detroit – Mackinac Island – St. Ignace – Chicago Division of D & C Lake Lines Pleasure Route to Vacation Land

"With a course lying around Lower Michigan, connecting the two chief cities of the midwest with the famous Mackinac Island resort area, this D. & C. line achieves increasing popularity each year.

Between June 30th and September 7th, three sailings per week are made from each port. Schedules are so arranged that within the span of a single week-end one can sail from Detroit or Chicago, to Mackinac Island, and return, combining with a visit to that northern vacation Mecca, a delightful 600-mile lake cruise.

The steamers *Eastern States* and *Western States* are assigned to this division. On board these pleasure-packed vessels splendid dance orchestras play each afternoon and evening. A social hostess is present to arrange introductions and direct social activities. Afternoon teas, bridge parties and deck sports…or big comfortable chairs out on the cool, breeze-swept decks…here are continued hours of happy activity, or of quiet restfulness, whichever the traveler most desires. One regrets the ending of these journeys."

-D & C Navigation Co., *Pleasure Days on the Blue Great Lakes, 1931*

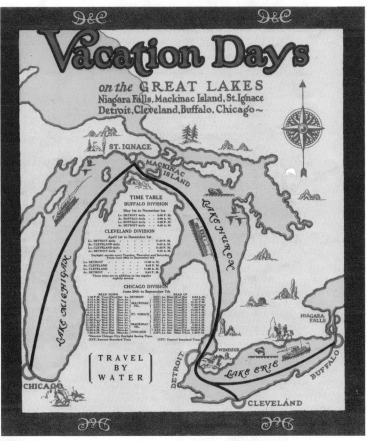

The Island Transportation Company

"This popular and well known concern…which plies daily between St. Ignace, Mackinac Island and Mackinaw City, connecting with all trains on the D.S. & A. R. R., the Michigan Central and the G.R. & I. R.R. The *Algomah* put in her appearance at the straits in October 1881; and was the first of the famous ice-crushers of this region. Her dimensions are 130 feet over all, 33 feet beam and 13 feet draught; with compound engine 19 x 30 and 36 inch stroke, and 1,000 indicated horse power. She accomplished good work whilst used for the purpose for which she was originally intended; is a safe and speedy craft; well equipped and excellently fitted up for the trade in which she is at present engaged. In addition to her regular traffic, the *Algomah* may be chartered during the season for pleasurable summer excursions to the various local points of interesting notoriety, and besides, is always kept in readiness for any wrecking or ice breaking service when needed by line steamers late in the fall season or in the early spring."

-City of St. Ignace and Mackinac County, for the Year 1895

Popular Side Trips to the Les Cheneaux Islands

"The Les Cheneaux Islands, about a hundred in number, lie clustered together in Lake Huron, near the mainland, some fourteen miles north and east of Mackinac. During the season, Arnold Line Steamers afford daily communication… Large numbers of bass, perch, muskellunge, Mackinaw trout, pickerel and pike are taken yearly from these waters… There are numerous small boats, both sail and rowing, for the accommodation of fishing parties, and competent guides to accompany, when desired. One can have a good day's sport and return to Mackinac Island the same evening in time for tea."

-Michigan Central R.R.,
Michigan Resorts, Chiefly in Northern Michigan, circa 1900

Grand Rapids & Indiana Railroad

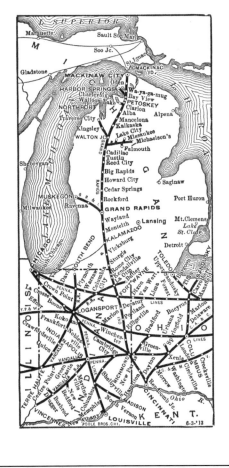

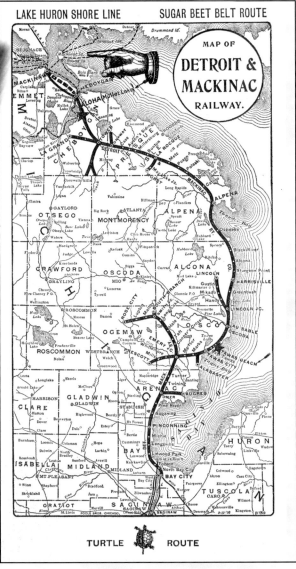

Travel by Rail

Railroads offered an alternative to steamship travel, and provided year-round service. The Grand Rapids & Indiana, Michigan Central, and the Detroit & Mackinac Railroads offered comfortable accommodations and frequent service for those traveling through the Lower Peninsula. Overnight travelers could leave sweltering cities such as Fort Wayne or Detroit and breathe the crisp air of the Straits by morning. The Duluth, South Shore and Atlantic Railroad offered service through the Upper Peninsula to St. Ignace. Train travel swelled in the summer season with hordes of tourists traveling to northern Michigan, Mackinac Island and the Upper Peninsula. The railroads promoted their service with advertising brochures and increased summer runs. The GR& I took on the slogan "the Fishing Line" and highlighted opportunities for fishing along its route. The D & M was a misnomer since it never actually reached Detroit or Mackinaw City, but ran from Bay City to Cheboygan. It was dubbed the "Sugar Beet Route" as it traveled through northeastern Michigan near the Lake Huron shore. Its advertising slogan was "the Turtle Route" since it heavily promoted travel to Mackinac Island, or "Turtle Island" as it was once known.

MICHIGAN CENTRAL RAILROAD
The N. Y. C. R. R. Co., Lessee

THE NIAGARA FALLS ROUTE

MICHIGAN CENTRAL R. R.
DETROIT
-TO-
MACKINAW CITY
Form 491-19 | Not Good If Detached
DESTINATION ST. IGNACE, Mich.
Issued by New York Central R. R.
Via NYC, MC, MTCo
If One-Half PunchHere
Baggage ★ PunchHere

Michigan Central – Favorite Tourist Route

"The Michigan Central has always been a favorite tourist route, both to the East and to the West, as well as to various Michigan resorts. Wherever its trains run, a pleasing panorama is presented to the passing traveler, to whose comfort and convenience its officials are never weary of administering. It has never spared care or expense in testing and adopting devices to diminish danger, insure safety, increase speed, or to add to its facilities…

The through sleepers of the Michigan Central operate in connection with the Grand Rapids & Indiana from Chicago, Harbor Springs and Mackinaw… At Mackinaw City, the terminus of the Mackinaw Division of the Michigan Central and also of the G.R. & I., the through sleeper from Detroit for Sault Ste. Marie is taken by car ferry to the old French mission settlement of St. Ignace, directly across the straits. Connection is made here with the D.S.S. & A. for Marquette, the Keweenaw Peninsula and Duluth."

- Michigan Central R.R., *Summer Vacation Tours,* 1910

MACKINAC ISLAND AND MICHIGAN RESORTS

Via MICHIGAN CENTRAL

THE NIAGARA FALLS ROUTE

NEW YORK CENTRAL LINES

SORENSON'S STANDARD SERVICE
MEATS, GROCERIES, ICE CREAM, SOFT DRINKS
ONE HALF MILE WEST OF FERRY DOCK, ON NEW U. S. 2
ST. IGNACE, MICH.

Vacationing Motorists

Traveling by automobile became a viable option to traveling by trains or steamships for many vacationers in the 1920s and 1930s. As automobiles became more affordable and vacation time more prevalent, more and more people traveled to their vacation destination by auto. Gas stations, restaurants hotels, rental cottages and campgrounds sprang up to meet the demands of these newly traveling vacationers. The tourist and resort industry rapidly expanded, especially in northern Michigan.

Improved road conditions, added road signage and road maps made travel by auto easier than it had been in the earlier days of motoring. Three of the state's main highways converged in Mackinaw City. The West Michigan Pike ran up the west side of the state, the East Michigan Pike ran up the east side, and the Mackinaw Trail passed through the middle of the Lower Peninsula. Thousands of motorists poured into the Straits area each summer. Some stayed in the region to vacation, others traveled into the Upper Peninsula or visited Mackinac Island.

Resort Property

"With the greatest demand for resort property that has ever been known, this is the time to buy lake frontage property. Prices are low, now. They cannot remain so, long. Good property, well located, will soon be unavailable except at high prices. The frontage on Lake Huron has already increased 100% and more... Summer homes sites right on Lake Huron can now be purchased at less cost than the smallest city lot. Whether you buy for your own summer home, or for investment, you will see a profit."

— *Mackinac Straits Shores,* circa 1926

Kellerest Cottage

Postcard message:

This is a view of our place. We are trying to get it fixed up. Been very busy all summer. At Mackinac Heights on the "Straits of Mackinac". Ten miles north of Cheboygan.

-August 22, 1939

Postcard not mailed.

Summer Homes and Cottages

People were drawn to the beauty of the Straits area and the wonderful recreational opportunities it offered. Many vacationers returned year after year and some built vacation homes. Developers foresaw the growing interest in the region and planned summer cottage communities to meet the demand for second homes. Mackinac Straits Shores, located on Lake Huron between Mackinaw City and Cheboygan, was developed in the 1920s. Mom-and-pop cabin courts came on the scene in the 1930s and 1940s. These sometimes-rustic cabins were very popular with vacationers and were often rented for a week or two. After World War II the postwar prosperity saw the explosion of both private summer homes and rental cottages scattered throughout the Straits region.

Chapter Two – Mackinaw City

Mackinaw City is located at the very "Tip of the Mitt," the northernmost point of the Lower Peninsula on the south shore of the Straits of Mackinac. It is one of the oldest settlements in Michigan. Its distinctive location has made it a center of trade and commerce throughout human history.

About 1714 the French built a mission and fur-trading compound at the site of Fort Michilimackinac, which served as a military trading post for most of the 17th century. The French traded with the Native Americans and established lasting relationships. The French voyageurs respected the culture of the Native Americans and some intermarried. In 1761, at the end of the French and Indian War, the British captured the fort. The British were not on good terms with the Native Americans, and unlike the French, considered them savages. In 1763 a plot was devised by Chief Pontiac to capture the fort. While playing baggatiway, a game similar to lacrosse, a ball was batted over the walls of the fort. Chasing the ball, the Native Americans gained admission and captured the fort. Most of the soldiers were massacred. The fort was reoccupied by the British in 1764 and abandoned in 1780 when a new fort was built on Mackinac Island, a more strategic location.

Although the garrison was moved to Mackinac Island, a small settlement outside the fort walls endured and eventually became Mackinaw City. Little is known of the history of the town from 1780 until 1857 when Edgar Conkling came to the area. Conkling surveyed the land and platted a village. He had the foresight to designate the site of the old fort as a public park. Conkling predicted that the settlement would be the "great central city" of the Straits region and become prosperous with mineral trade, fishing and lumbering; it would be the "Venice of the Lakes," rich with beauty and culture.

Despite these impressive predictions, there was no development until 1869 when Conkling built a dock at Mackinaw City. The next year George Stimpson and his family settled in the village and developed a business supplying cordwood to the steamers passing through the Straits. He built the Stimpson House, the first hotel in the village. The Michigan Central Railroad arrived in 1881, followed by the Grand Rapids & Indiana Railroad in 1882. The village was incorporated that same year. The railroads brought in new settlers and new commercial enterprises and the village developed over the next few decades. By the 1920s Mackinaw City was an active railroad terminal with as many as twenty passenger trains, and numerous freight trains, arriving at the depot daily.

Industry never really took hold in Mackinaw City. Its economy has been anchored in tourism, which started to develop about 1900. The old fort site was designated Michilimackinac State Park in 1909. The new park didn't see much activity until three major highways converged at Mackinaw City. In 1913 the state's highways were mapped out by the new Michigan State Highway Department. The West Michigan Pike ran up the west side of the state, the East Michigan Pike ran up the east side and the Mackinaw Trail cut through the middle of the Lower Peninsula. These state highways brought thousands of vacationing motorists to Mackinaw City each summer. The city's entrepreneurs responded by creating services that catered to the needs of these travelers.

Auto travel was given a boost in 1923 when the State Highway Department started car ferry service across the Straits. A ferry dock was built at Mackinaw City and was improved and expanded over the years. The ferry service also brought jobs and publicity, stimulating the economy.

Summer vacationers were attracted to the natural beauty of the area and many summer homes were built. Some resorters came for relief from hay fever and asthma. Wawatam Beach, a large cottage colony on the shores of the Straits, was developed in the early 1900s. Numerous mom-and-pop rental cabins and cottages were built in the area to house itinerant tourists and summer vacationers.

The modern era of Mackinaw City began in 1957 when the Mackinac Bridge opened. New hotels, motels, restaurants and souvenir shops were opened to service the throngs of tourists. Michilimackinac State Park was used as a campground until historic restoration was started in 1959. Since then, the fort has been returned to its 1763 appearance, encompassing military quarters, a church, homes of French traders and other structures. Besides the historic Fort Michilimackinac, Mackinaw City has other attractions including sandy beaches, swimming, boating, fishing, and excellent shops and restaurants. Visitors today are just as impressed with the picturesque views of Mackinac Island from the shores of Mackinaw City, as were those earlier generations of travelers.

Study This Map, the More You Study It, the More You Will Be Intrigued With What This Part of Michigan Has to Offer.

The Tip of the Mitt

"Mackinaw City is the northern terminus of two arterial highways, at the uppermost tip of the Lower Peninsula. Each summer is bright and busy and crowded with tourists, who swarm through the village on their way to the Upper Peninsula. Year-round ferries, crossing the Straits of Mackinac to St. Ignace, use the ornate dock maintained by the State."

-Writers' Program of the W.P.A., *Michigan: a Guide to the Wolverine State,* 1941

Mackinaw City

"Mackinaw is an incorporated village on the most northerly point of the Lower Peninsula, in the township of Mackinaw, Cheboygan County, on the Michigan Central Railroad, the Grand Rapids & Indiana Railway Division of the Pennsylvania System and the Duluth, South Shore & Atlantic Railroad…. It has gained great popularity as a summer resort, owing to its beautiful and romantic surroundings and its bracing air. It is lighted by electricity, and has a bank, a public library, a number of hotels for the accommodations of resorters, Catholic, Methodist and Presbyterian churches and a good school."

-Polk, R. L. & Co., *Michigan Gazetteer*, 1921

Postcard message:

I am sending you a postcard
With just a line or two
To say that I'm at Mackinaw City
And thinking of you.

Postmarked Mackinaw, 1919
Mailed to Saginaw, Mich.

Stop Over at Mackinaw City

"FISHING: Brook and Lake Trout. White Fish, Bass and Perch.

HUNTING: Deer and small game.

BOATING: Steamer and Speed Boats to Mackinac Island, Les Cheneaux Islands, Upper Peninsula. Also canoeing and sailing.

BATHING: Safe, shallow, warm water and sand beaches.

GOLFING: One of America's most scenic Golf Courses, well laid-out and maintained.

STATE TOURIST CAMP: Thirty acres on the water's edge of the Straits, with tall Pine and Birch shelter, fine turf, running water, and modern conveniences.

BY LAND, WATER, OR AIR: Mackinaw City is in reality not a city at all. The noise and nerve strain of City life is replaced in 'Old Mackinaw' by that quaint, restful atmosphere found along the sea coast villages of New England with a more colorful setting and as much historical background.

MACKINAW CITY: Is easily reached by boat, rail and auto. It is the terminal for three railroads: the Michigan Central, the Pennsylvania, and the D.S.S. & A.
US-31 and US-23 lead directly to the 'Monument' which is located at the apex of the East Michigan Pike, Dixie Highway and the Mackinaw Trail. You may even come by air to the Mackinaw City Airport which is only a matter of two miles from town."

-Mackinaw City Chamber of Commerce,
Stop Over at Mackinaw City, Michigan, circa 1935

17

Dixie Highway Monument

"…Tomorrow's event marks the unveiling of the monument dedicating the consummation of the enterprise connecting the Dixie Highway from Miami, Florida, with the West Michigan and East Michigan pikes. The shaft is located at the apex of the great highway facing the Straits of Mackinac opposite Mackinac Island. It is composed of stones gathered by citizens from all parts of the country, some coming from far away Alaska. The shaft is 15 feet high. On one side is the inscription 'The West Michigan Pike' and on the other 'The East Michigan Pike.' While at the top is an attractive arrow pointing southward marked 'The Dixie Highway.' On the base of the monument is the inscription, 'Dedicated to Horatio S. Earle, Father of Good Roads in Michigan.' Mr. Earle will be a distinguished figure in the unveiling ceremonies."

-*Grand Rapids Herald*, July 14, 1916

Postcard message:

This highway monument is where the highways meet at the "Tip of the Mitt". We stayed here Aug. 2, 1926 on our way back from Sault. Ste. Marie. Mackinaw City is the last north city on the Lower Peninsula.
Susan & Hazel

Postmarked Mackinaw, 1926
Mailed to Kalamazoo, Mich.

Place Now a Tourist Town

"The entire Straits region is rich in history and romance. The section upon which the modern Mackinaw City stands is endowed with a background of historical interest that would be difficult to equal anywhere in North America. Motor tourists from Indiana and Texas, who drive up to the state dock to wait for a ferry to the other side, gaze out upon the same Straits and upon the same Mackinac Island as did Father Marquette. Many a camper at the state park spends the night but a stone's throw away from the scene of the massacre of the English garrison.

Mackinaw City is primarily a tourist town. Its location has made it so. The lower peninsula is shaped roughly like a funnel, with the small spout end at Mackinaw City. Roads which begin at the very outer rim of the funnel top – for instance, Detroit and Chicago, two hundred miles or more apart – converge at Mackinaw City, as do many other trunk lines which traverse the state in a north and south direction. During the summer months, it is estimated that more tourists are concentrated in this region than at any other point in the United States.

With the development of the automobile and the evolution of the motor tourist taking place but a comparatively short time ago, the business men of Mackinaw City found it necessary to adapt themselves to changing conditions and today practically all commercial activity is aimed toward the tourist trade. Good hotels and restaurants are to be found on every hand. First-class mercantile establishments are at the disposal of the summer visitor...

Two railroads – the Pennsylvania and Michigan Central – have their northern terminals at Mackinaw City. Ferry service across the Straits of Mackinac is adequate to serve both the railroads and the motor traffic. The business institutions of the town make every effort to serve and please the tourists who halt there on their way north or south."

-Emmet County Graphic, September 10, 1925

MAIN STREET, MACKINAW CITY, MICH.   117991

"Mackinaw City Popular Place
Tourists Like it Right on Shore of Straits of Mackinac

This little upper Michigan watering place, located at the most northern tip of the lower peninsula, is just now being visited by more automobile parties from more different places in the country than any other spot in Michigan. The beautiful state park on the shores of the straits and the ferry wharf, are, of course, the main points where those visiting cars are found. Thousands who planned to 'go right on through' are so pleased with the village that they stay here for extended visits. Those who were here last year, find many changes made, many more attractive little shops and nooks to spend their time. Many more summer places to house the guests, more spots to watch the fishermen, etc. are also found. There have been a lot of guests lately at the park."

-Petoskey Evening News, July 18, 1929

Center of Commerce

Mackinaw City became the center of commerce for the "Tip of the Mitt." Businesses served both the local and tourist populations. In 1927 the West Michigan Tourist Association compiled a survey and found that most tourists needed to buy vacation essentials on the road. Popular purchases included camping gear, sporting gear, bathing suits, cameras and compasses. These items were purchased in addition to the regular supplies of food and gasoline. Wise entrepreneurs saw the need for restaurants, grocery stores, gift and souvenir shops, gasoline stations and automobile garages that catered to the needs of travelers.

Postcard message:

Tues. morning
Dearest Kiddies,
Well we are all packed up and ready for the home stretch. We are waiting here in Mac. City for the hardware store to open so I can get a little remembrance, so when we get home, I will really know that we have been to the Straits. Ha!

- Lovingly, Ma & Pa

Postmarked Mackinaw City, date not legible
Mailed to St. Louis, Mich.

Good Hotels

"Mackinaw has gained great popularity as a summer resort, owing to its beautiful and romantic surroundings and its bracing air. It has a number of good hotels for the accommodation of resorters, the largest and best of these is the Stimpson House."

-Polk, R. L. & Co., *Michigan Gazetteer,* 1901

STIMPSON HOUSE, MACKINAW CITY, MICH.

STIMPSON HOUSE

D. SMITH & SON, Proprietors

Rates, American Plan—$2 per day, Special Weekly $10 to $12

Bar stocked with Finest Wines and Liquors.
Steam Heat.   Electric Light.   Inside Toilets.
Open every day in the year.   Convenient to all Trains and Boats.
Particular attention to Commercial Men and Summer Visitors.
Only Commercial Hotel in the City.

MACKINAW CITY   -   MICH.

The Old Fashioned Inn

"We Serve a Special Dinner of Mackinaw White Fish and Trout for $1.00. Satisfaction Assured, Automobile parties and Tourists Solicited. Central Avenue at Lake. Newell & Dodd Props."

-Polk, R.L. & Co., *Michigan Gazetteer,* 1923

Postcard message:

Dear Auntie,
This is where I'm spending my
vacation. Couldn't you please write.
        -A.C. c/o Old Fashioned Inn
        Mackinaw City, Mich.

Postmarked Mackinaw, 1928
Mailed to Ada, Mich.

Hotel Windermere

"A small comfortable resort for particular people directly on the Straits of Mackinac, nearby all docks, stations, theater, restaurants, stores, gift shops, just off highways. Large car storage. Ample parking space free. Landscaped gardens. Private beach. All sports. Write for free photo-cards and hotel rates (day, week or month). A.H. Cheney, Mackinaw City, Mich. Phone 2021 or 9131."

-West Michigan Tourist Association,
Carefree Days in West Michigan, 1950

HOTEL WINDERMERE

Directly on the water
at the Straits of Mackinac

MACKINAW CITY

A friendly, family hotel, ideally located. European plan, very reasonable rates. Pleasant, airy rooms with double or twin beds, many with private bath. Colonial Dining Room, cheerful lobby, large porches and lawns.

For reservations, write A. H. Cheney,
owner - operator

Postcard message:

Monday Eve.
Dear Hattie,
We hope you are feeling much better now. We are staying in Mackinaw City tonight. Having a nice trip. Took a boat ride through the Soo Locks yesterday and a long ferry ride trip across the straits of Mackinac. Will be home in a few days.
*   -Love and Best Wishes, Joyce & Al*

Postmarked Mackinac City, 1948
Mailed to Painted Post, N.Y.

Enjoyable Visits

"Within Mackinaw City are many outstanding hotels, overnight cabins, cottages and tourist homes...dining rooms, restaurants and roadside eating places, and a hundred other services to make the tourists' visit enjoyable."

-West Michigan Tourist Association,
Carefree Days in West Michigan, 1951

Postcard message;

We are spending 2 nites in this hotel. I wish you could see the interesting things we've seen. Tomorrow at 7:00 a.m. we'll leave for Sault St. Marie. We'll see about leaving there in the p.m. – this is a swell trip as ever.
-Ella

Postmarked Mackinaw City, 1950
Mailed to Lake Mills, Wis.

Hotel Manitou

"Twenty-eight rooms with and without baths. Rates: $3.00-$6.00 single per day and $4.00-$10.00 double per day. European plan. Meals. Cocktail Lounge. Open May 1 to December 1. Ferris L. Coffman, Mackinaw City, Mich, Phone 3601."

-East Michigan Tourist Association, *Playtime Guide Book,* 1955

"Newest Tourist Camp is Opened
Very Most Modern Plan for Touring Folk is Ready at Mackinaw

Something new and modern in the way of tourist camps has been established at Mackinaw City and is known as 'Sids's Cottages and Tourist Camp.'

The tourist cabins form a semicircle which partly surround the main building, which is a store for supplies, a large lobby for the guests of the camp and a fine dining room, where the guests of the camp may procure their meals. There are sixteen cottages, all of which are electrically lighted, have hot and cold running water and in general are the finest type of tourist over-night cabins seen anywhere. On the premise is also a shower bath for men and one for women which is another added attraction. To the rear of these is a large camp ground with many shade trees in the natural woods. All of the buildings are screened to assure the guests that insects will not molest them during their stay.

The main building accommodates a spacious lobby with a beautiful fireplace, lounges, writing tables and other comforts and conveniences for the tourists. The dining room which joins the lobby is tastefully decorated and is something new for such a tourist camp. The store room is to the right of the lobby and is stocked with merchandise that a tourist would want to purchase.

Each of the many cabins are named in memory of some Indian tribe which visited Mackinaw or for some of the early priests who first came to Mackinaw."

-Petoskey Evening News, June 12, 1930

Sid's
Mackinaw City

Sid's Red and White Cottages
Mackinaw, Michigan
Home of Mackinaw Trout
Sixteen cottages, each containing good beds, hot and cold water and small stove. Lunch room, dining room, community room for use of guests. All the features of a club. Showers for ladies and men.
Specialty — Chicken and Fish Dinners
Gas and Oil station. Good bathing, sandy beach. Golf. Confections, Ice Cream, Cigars, Cigarettes, Soft Drinks.
Camping grounds among the pines and white birches, is supplied with city water, electric lights.
Also a camp house for bad weather. Fishing in nearby lakes, big lake perch are caught off the pier.

Sid's Red & White Cottages
and
Camp Ground

The Breakers Tourist Cabins, Mackinaw City, Michigan.

Postcard message:

Thursday,
Hello Folks-
Wish you were here today. The lake is full of "White Caps" and the sky is so blue. We can see the lake from our cabin. This is a picture of where we are.
Our best- Jack & Elaine

Postmarked Mackinac City, 1947
Mailed to Tecumseh, Mich.

The Breakers Tourist Cabins

"Located at the State Ferry Dock, Mackinaw City. Terminal of US-31-27-23-131. Twenty units accommodating 70 guests. All cabins equipped with running water, electric stoves for cooking and stoves for heat. Bathing beach and spacious lawn where you can rest, play shuffleboard, croquet and other games. Good beds. Fourteen cabins have private toilets. Community showers. Restaurant and garage nearby. Rates $1.00 single; double $1.50 and up. Day, week, month. Mrs. Ella B. Phillips, manager."

Recognized Tourist Cabin Camp Guide, 1941

Pontiac Lodge

"Located on US-23, 300 feet from intersection of US-31 and US-27. Overlooking the Straits of Mackinac. Eighteen all modern cabins, with private showers and private flush toilets. Lodge and cabin accommodations for 80 guests. Best of beds. Duo-Therm oil heat, insulated. Lounge room in the Lodge with radio and fireplace. Fine dining room, specializing in Steaks, Chicken and Fish. Also lunches, cold drinks, and breakfasts. Pleasant surroundings. Rates $2.00 up. Ray and Katherine Martin."

-Recognized Tourist Cabin Camp Guide, 1941

Postcard message:

Hello folks. Did you survive that heat wave – it was bad for us northerners also, but cold today – have fire in range. I was in Cheboygan yesterday, ten miles from here – such cars, the highway has been full all summer.
Glad to get your letter – come again for a visit.

-M.B.B.

Postmarked Mackinac City, 1939
Mailed to Grand Rapids, Mich.

Millinac Cabins

"Located on the Straits of Mackinac, US-23 and 27 and just east of US-31. Thirty-three units, accommodating 90 guests. Hot and cold running water. Private flush toilets, private bath. Also community showers and toilets. Cooking accommodations and restaurant nearby. Private beach. Landscaped grounds, well-lighted, modern bedding equipment. Ten units with screened porches. Single rates $1.50 up; double rates $3.00 up. Douglas Miller, manager."

-Recognized Tourist Cabin Camp Guide, 1941

Postcard message:

Wed. morning
Our cabin is located two blocks from the state ferry Docks. It is
one grand parade of boats past here. Hay fever letting up and will
be starting home the last of the week. Will see you Monday. Best
Wishes.

-Clark

Postmarked Mackinaw City, 1942
Mailed to Jonesville, Mich.

Patrick's Cabins on the Straits

"Two blocks south of State Ferry Docks; one block north of Junction US-23, 27 and 31. Each cabin has heat, running water, toilet and showers, privacy, comfortable beds with innerspring mattresses, bathing beach, electricity. From the cabins you can watch the procession of lake boats passing."

-East Michigan Tourist Association, Eat-Sleep-Shop in East Michigan, 1941

Waneta Cabins – Cottages

"Located at the city limits of Mackinaw City, on the Straits of Mackinac – overlooking historic Mackinac Island. Just south of junction US-31 and on Highway US-23 and US-27. One mile south of State Ferry Dock. 38 new, modern, insulated cottages, heated. 38 bathrooms. 31 cottages have electric equipped kitchenettes, hot and cold showers in each cottage. Rustic furniture, the best of beds and latest modern sleeping equipment. Private beach. Day or week at moderate rates. Phone 3481. Box 465. Mr. And Mrs. H.F. Loeffler."

-Recognized Tourist Cabin Camp Guide, 1941

Postcard message:

Believe Michigan is your vacation spot. We are certainly enjoying ourselves. Fishing, swimming and sightseeing. Have a nice cottage at Mackinaw City. Leave here in the morning to cross over by ferry to the Northern Peninsula.

Love, Grace

Postmarked Mackinaw City, 1948
Mailed to East Cleveland, Ohio

TEYSEN'S
MACKINAW
CITY
MICH.

2141

"Teysen Original Frontier Restaurant is Feature of Mackinaw City

One of the most unique and interesting places to visit on the Straits of Mackinac is the Teysen Original Frontier Restaurant at Mackinaw City.

Mr. and Mrs. Teysen came north some fifteen years ago, after remarkable hotel success in southern Michigan, and built their somewhat different Indian restaurant on the lake front at Mackinaw City. It quickly commanded the attention and patronage of the public, and today its fame and friends extend from coast to coast. Artists have studied and copied the interior of this 'Original Frontier' building, and its museum and curio department attract thousands of tourists.

No better meals are served anywhere than those brought to guests at Teysen's by the genuine Indian maids who serve as waitresses. They come year after year from Indian schools, and receive the personal care and attention of Mrs. Teysen.

A complete information service is maintained, as well as a unique historical free museum inside the stockade of Fort Michlimackinac on the Straits shore.

Famous men and women are among the Teysen patrons, and their names have been gratefully written on the heads of the Indian drums which adorn this remarkable building."

-Mackinac Island News, August 2, 1940

TEYSEN'S
MACKINAW CITY, MICHIGAN

Postcard message:

9/3/1948
This place is just full of beautiful Indian gifts. Came up M-23 all the way.
Drove 348 miles Friday. Took our time. Stayed at Cheboygan Fri. night.
Nice cabins, just fun to cook and do we ever eat! Spent an hour at the old
fort this morning. Going on 11:00am ferry across the Straits and then to
the Soo. Wish you could have come with us.

-Ruby & Les

Postmarked Mackinaw City, 1948
Mailed to Elsie, Mich.

WINDMILL WAFFLE SHOP — MACKINAW CITY, MICH.   6A91-N

Waffle Shop Has Steady Patronage

"The Windmill Waffle Shop at Mackinaw City enjoys the reputation of being one of the most unusual eating places to be found anywhere. The place is located but a short distance from the railroad depot and at the same time is conveniently accessible to the railroad ferry dock…

The Windmill Waffle Shop is owned and operated by Mrs. Cora B. Andrews. It takes its name from a genuine Dutch windmill and tower that are part of the building. The huge blades of the windmill may be seen for miles when approaching Mackinaw City by boat.

The restaurant itself is charmingly appointed and immaculate in its appearance. Tasty decorations give it an atmosphere of refinement seldom attained in a place of its kind. It gives the impression of being a high-class place in every respect. Service is by highly trained waitresses. Cooks are expert in their art, and an air of hospitality pervades the place."

-*Petoskey Evening News*, August 7, 1930

Wegner's Café

"Wegners Café, on US-23, 27 and 31, opposite Breaker Cabins, two toilets, hot and cold water, meals served year round, lake 100 yards. Fish and Steak Dinners, safe bathing beach nearby."

-East Michigan Tourist Association,
Eat-Sleep Places in East Michigan, circa 1940

Wegner's Cafe, Mackinaw City, Mich.   9A-H1974

Postcard message:

Hello Helen & Jack,
We arrived all OK. Drove up in twelve hours from home. Car perfect. This is surely the place to rest. I slept fourteen hours last night – just what I needed. Ray is fishing now. We'll see you next week.
-Gladys & Ray

Postmarked Mackinaw City, 1940
Mailed to Columbus, Ohio

Postcard message:

We are just having breakfast at Mackinaw City. No trouble on the trip up. Brrrr! It's cold up here this morning. We are going to the Soo Locks since we made such good time so far. There are lots of nice cabins here for you to stay overnite, but we decided to stay in a hotel, since we got here so late.

-Bessie

Postmarked Mackinaw City, 1952
Mailed to Cleveland, Ohio

Fine Fish Dinners

"The Straits of Mackinac are the native home of the White Fish and Mackinaw Trout. One should not miss the fine fish dinners while in our territory."

-Mackinaw City Chamber of Commerce,
Stop Over at Mackinaw City, Michigan, circa 1935

GREYHOUND POST HOUSE MACKINAW CITY, MICH.

GREYHOUND POST HOUSE-MACKINAW CITY, MICH.

Native Materials Go Into New Mackinaw Bus Station

"Pine logs from sand dunes west of St. Ignace and rock from quarries near Onaway went into the building of the $100,000 Greyhound bus terminal at Mackinaw City which opened recently…

The building is constructed in a fort style with a blockhouse over the main entrance on the southeast corner facing the car ferry docks.

Inside the log building the Greyhound Post House occupies the main section – a beamless room that measures 175 by 39 feet. The Post House serves meals both cafeteria and restaurant style to passengers on the incoming buses.

A stone fireplace which reaches 32 feet high is on the east end of the building and will be used during the winter months. Also in the main part of the building are the ticket office, information booth and souvenir shop.

Radiant heat for the building is supplied through 6,000 feet of pipes laid under the quarry tile floor.

Buses are loaded in the concourse located on the north end of the building. Between the concourse and the main room there is a connecting hallway leading to the baggage room, drivers' quarters, men and women's restrooms, finished in western panel cedar, celetex block ceiling and a tile floor.

The kitchen, located in the rear of the building, has modern equipment and is finished in both wall and floor tile.

A garage that will house ten buses is in the rear of the building. Windows in the station are of thermopane glass, resistant to both heat and cold.

Work still to be completed includes black-topping the driveways of the terminal, laying out of a parking lot, and the installation of a double Greyhound sign on the roof of the concourse. The neon sign will measure 18 by 31 feet and will feature the Greyhound hound racing. One sign will face the highway going south while the other will face the Straits…"

-*Petoskey Evening News*, August 2, 1947

Entrance to Michilimakinac State Park, Mackinaw City, Mich.

"Tourists Lounge in Quiet State Park at Mackinaw City

The old fort site at Mackinaw City, now a state park, has been provided with accessories necessary to the comfort of those stopping at the end of the two pikes. There is a big stone stove with iron top large enough for a number of parties of campers and picnickers to use at once, and really picturesque in appearance. There is a pavilion with tables, as well as tables in the open, a convenient pump and other facilities for making camp easy. A register to be signed by visitors to the park, which is placed in a box attached to a tree, is already quite filled with names of tourists from all over this state and a few from other states.

It is indeed pleasant to eat lunch in the shade of the grand old trees and afterward wander over to the lighthouse to watch the stately ships go by on their way to the Soo or Mackinac Island, that on clear days seem but a step away. As darkness comes on bringing out the lights of the Grand Hotel til they gleam like diamonds…

Within the park are swings and chutes for the little children to play while perhaps the older ones may be attracted to wander on to the less frequented western part of the park…"

-*Grand Rapids Herald*, August 15, 1920

Postcard message:

We would love to picnic here. Too cool for us tonight so we are in a hotel. Drove over 300 miles today. Start back tomorrow afternoon and will be home by Tuesday.

-*Jessie*

Postmarked Mackinaw, 1929
Mailed to Cleveland, Ohio

Michilimackinac State Park, Mackinaw City, Mich.

Michilimackinac State Park

"The pure water of artesian wells, the fragrance of balsam, fir, and the beauty of clusters of white birch, together with the heavy turf covering the ground, make this an ideal camping place. There is a small charge for camping."

-Mackinaw City Chamber of Commerce,
Stop Over at Mackinaw City, circa 1935

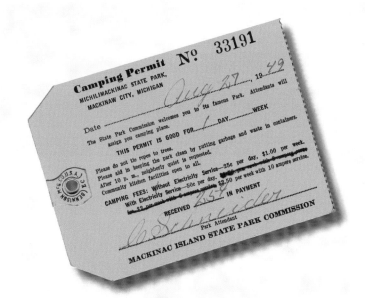

Postcard message:

Tuesday. All O.K. Are going to camp here. 443 miles from home. Aunt Margaret was fascinated by this lighthouse, a short walk from our camp. Had pork and beans for dinner.

Dad & Mother

Postmarked Mackinaw, date not legible
Mailed to Elkhart, Ind

Postcard message:

Hello Larry – Here is where we are camping and wouldn't you like to be here. Having a good time and expect to be home Sunday. We are going on a boat ride tomorrow to Mackinac Island and St. Ignace.
Goodbye from Grandma & Grandpa

Postmarked Mackinaw City, 1941
Mailed to Litchfield, Mich.

Fort Michilimackinac

"The old Fort and Stockade has been rebuilt upon the old foundations, giving the exact location and shape, as near a duplicate of the original as possible, to perpetuate the memory of the old Fort Michilimackinac, the most historic spot in the entire Northwest.

An Indian family lives in the stockade during the summer, making souvenir and baskets for sale, and entertaining visitors with stories of their life and customs."

-Mackinaw City Chamber of Commerce,
Stop Over at Mackinaw City, circa 1935

Postcard message:

8/30/30
Dear Mother,
Well, I'm feeling all right again. I guess I caught a cold riding the ferry boat. I guess we will leave Mackinaw in a couple of days, and start down the lake shore. Dad and I both put on a new set of clothes this morning. Guess we will go after huckleberries today. See you in a week.

Harold

Postmarked Mackinaw, 1930
Mailed to Middleville, Mich.

Postcard message:

Hi,
Sure was hot traveling today. Took our time because we weren't in any
hurry. Went thru the fort this afternoon. The boys got a bang out of it.
They're swimming now.

Love, Harriet

Posttmarked Mackinaw City, 1962
Mailed to Benton Harbor, Mich.

Authentic Restoration

"The fort and its buildings, the exhibits, period settings, and all the other historical features you see during your tour are the result of the most careful research of trained archaeologists and historians to make this one of America's most completely authentic reconstructions.

Fort Michilimackinac's reconstruction had been financed entirely by revenue bonds which are paid off by admission fees. No tax money had been used in the reconstruction, which began in 1959."

-Mackinac Island State Park Commission,
Historic Fort Michilimackinac, circa 1965

Postcard message:

Mackinaw City.

Aug. 11th

Dear Auntie: We arrived here last Friday morning. Are enjoying the "simple life." The air is doing me much good and I feel stronger already. Mother is gradually getting rested too. Expect a girlfriend to visit tomorrow. Wish you could come too. It seems so good to be where it is quiet. With love from all of us.

Angie

Postmarked Mackinaw, 1910
Mailed to Woodbury, Mich.

Where have I been?
Renewing my youth at
Wawatam Inn.

WAWATAM INN, MACKINAW CITY, MICHIGAN

Postcard message:

9-14-1914
We reached here a week ago last night after a delightful trip on the lake.
Found eight or nine at the cottages that we had met before so we had a jolly
time. The "sneezers" are gradually leaving for their homes, went down to the
dock early this morning to see several off. Only four of us left. I don't know
when we'll leave.

-Mary

Postmarked Mackinaw, 1914
Mailed to Marietta, Ohio

Interesting History

"Students of History and Old Folk Lore find much material for study as they vacation here. Students of Wildlife, Anthropology, and Archaeology roam our shores and trails continually. Authors of historical books and authors of frontier fiction find much material to use as they visit with old timers and Indian Chiefs who live in the neighborhood."

-Mackinaw City Chamber of Commerce,
Chief of all Vacation Places Invites You to Mackinaw City, Michigan, circa 1930

Postcard message:

Mackinaw, August 18, 1926
Dear Donald,
We arrived last night. Stayed with Ella. Am feeling better.
Think this trip will do us good. I just bought this card
from the old chief himself. He looks just like the picture.
                    Love to all, Papa

Postmarked Mackinaw, 1926
Mailed to Grandville, Mich.

Mackinaw Headlands Golf Course

"Mackinaw Headlands Golf Course offers its attractions to lovers of this sport. Its wonderful location on the hills south of Mackinaw gives a view of the entire Straits region, the passing of boats, the panoramic view of islands of the Straits, cool breezes, and the wild beauty of the grounds add to the attractiveness of this nine-hole course. It is the only course in Michigan which has this ground rule: 'If the ball lands in a deer track, the ball can be moved.' It is not an uncommon sight to see deer on the grounds."

-Mackinaw City Chamber of Commerce,
Stop Over at Mackinaw City, circa 1933

No.1 Fairway, Mackinaw Headlands Golf Course. Mackinaw City, Mich.

Postcard message:

Sept. 5

Dear Folks,

We are back in Mackinaw again. Have been having a wonderful time. Wish you were here with us. My golf game has improved slightly.

Love, Ruth

Postmarked Mackinaw, 1930
Mailed to Chicago, Illinois

Chapter Three- Crossing the Straits: the Car Ferries

The original ferry service across the Straits of Mackinac transported railroad cars. In 1881 the three railroads that serviced the Straits formed the Mackinac Transportation Company. The *Algomah* was the first steamship to run between Mackinaw City and St. Ignace. It was followed by the *St. Ignace,* the *Sainte Marie* and the *Chief Wawatam.* Later these railroad ferries carried automobiles along with train cars, but the service was inadequate, infrequent and quite expensive. As more and more motorists traveled to the Straits, more efficient ferry service was demanded by the public.

In 1923 the Michigan Legislature established car ferry service at the Straits, giving the State Highway Department responsibility for operating ferry service between Mackinaw City and St. Ignace. The State purchased a dock at St. Ignace and arranged temporary use of the Michigan Central Railroad dock at Mackinaw City on a rental basis. A dock site was purchased later about 500 feet south of the railroad dock.

The first State car ferry was the steamer *Ariel,* a small river ferry which had plied the Detroit River. The boat had a 16-20 automobile capacity. She made her first trip in July 1923 and was laid up the following November. She could not handle the rough waters of the Straits and was sold in 1924 for service on the St. Clair River.

In that same year the State purchased two boats, the *Colonel Card* and the *Colonel Pond,* from the U.S. Government for $15,000 each. The boats were renamed the *St. Ignace* and the *Mackinaw City* and were enlarged from 130 feet to 180 feet, thus creating a capacity for 40 cars each. The traffic across the Straits increased so rapidly that during the winter of 1925-26 the boats were again enlarged by adding eight feet on each side, increasing the capacity for each to carry between 55 and 60 cars.

Business continued to increase and in 1928 a third boat, the *Straits of Mackinac,* was added to the fleet. This boat was specifically built for the State Highway Department and had a capacity for about 60 cars. This third boat did much to relieve the annoying delays suffered by motorists the previous years, but traffic continued to grow and the following year an upper deck was added to the *Straits of Mackinac.* In 1930 a similar deck was added to the *Mackinaw City.* During the summer of 1930 a popular night schedule was added.

Service further improved in 1931 when the dock at Mackinaw City was rebuilt to permit three boats to load at once. An elevator was added for loading the upper decks of the car ferries. The following year the dock at St. Ignace was expanded and an elevator added. Parking facilities were added in 1937.

Traffic in the Straits area continued to increase as the Depression eased. The State purchased the former railroad car ferry, the *Ann Arbor IV.* She was extensively remodeled and renamed the *City of Cheboygan.* She had a capacity for 85 cars and began her duties in the summer of 1937. The next ferry added to the fleet was another railroad car ferry, the *Pere Marquette No. 20,* purchased by the State in 1938. She was renamed the *City of Munising* and had a stern-loading capacity for 105 cars.

In 1940 the U.S. Government bought back the *Mackinaw City* and the *St. Ignace* as part of the national defense arsenal. The State Highway Department acted quickly and purchased the *Pere Marquette 17,* with a capacity for 105 cars, and renamed her the *City of Petoskey.* She was reconditioned and started service in time for the 1940 deer-hunting season. Traffic at the Straits decreased during the war as gas rationing went into effect.

The postwar years saw a steady increase in traffic at the Straits and a greater need for improved ferry service. The *City of Cheboygan,* the *City of Munising,* and the *City of Petoskey* had improvements made during the winter of 1946-47. Their bows were cut down and forward loading ramps built. The boats could now save ten minutes on each trip since they no longer had to back up to the docks.

Serious discussion of building a bridge across the Straits was now taking place. Highway Commissioner, Charles Ziegler, was opposed to a bridge and wanted to see the ferry service expanded. Against strong opposition from bridge advocates, Ziegler succeeded in adding a new icebreaker ferry, the *Vacationland,* in 1952. A new dock was built at St. Ignace to accommodate the large ship, which could carry 150 cars and trucks. The fleet now had a capacity for carrying 500 vehicles, but even that wasn't enough to meet the demand and the ferry service only lasted a few years longer.

When the Mackinac Bridge opened in November 1957, the car ferry service was put out of commission. The boats were offered for sale. The docks were leased to private ferry companies offering service to Mackinac Island. During its reign of 34 years the State ferry service carried approximately 12 million vehicles and 30 million travelers across the scenic Straits of Mackinac.

CHIEF WAWATAM, Railway Ferry,
Straits of Mackinac, Mich.

G.H. Wickman, Publisher.   Made in Germany

Hello Kate:
This is the boat we loaded Lizzie on to cross the
Straits. Drove right up the railroad track. We
surely have seen some roads! We took a trip by
boat from St. Ignace to the Soo. We are having the
time of our lives. We are in the solid timber about
25 miles from any town. Tell the boys Lizzie has
been quite a curiosity to people. Night before last
ice froze 1/2 inch thick. Lots of huckleberries
froze. We have had all we want to eat.

Postmarked Seney, 1917
Mailed to Sunfield, Mich.

Chief Wawatam

"Steamer *Chief Wawatam*, which went into commission on the St. Ignace – Mackinaw City run in the fall of 1911, is the largest and best equipped steel car-ferry in the world. According to the officials of the Mackinac Transportation Co., who owns her, she is 352 feet over all and can carry 25 standard length cars. Her engines of 5,000 H.P. drive her at a speed of 18 miles per hour. Was built by the Toledo Ship Building Co., Toledo, Ohio."

-Postcard back, circa 1912

Highway Department Operates Ferry Boats

"One of the activities of the highway department of the state of Michigan which has an important effect upon the recreational history which the state is writing, is the operation of a ferry service between Mackinaw City in the Lower Peninsula and St. Ignace in the Upper Peninsula.

The service is an extension of the Michigan system of highways. The state highway department operates these ferries to carry tourists and others together with their cars expeditiously and economically between the two peninsulas. Before the state embarked upon this marine enterprise, tourists and cars were carried across the Straits of Mackinac on railroad ferries at some inconvenience to travelers because rails on the boats were troublesome obstacles to negotiate and because the time schedules caused delays.

The state inaugurated its experiment in 1923 by purchasing a dock in St. Ignace, renting the Michigan Central dock at Mackinaw City and purchasing a single boat. This boat, the *Ariel*, made its first trip July 31, 1923, and was laid up in November.

In the fall of 1923, the state purchased two boats from the federal government. The boats cost the federal government $300,000 each and were sold (or given) to the state for $15,000 each. They were 130 feet long and had beams of 28 feet. They were lengthened to 180 feet, which gave them each a capacity of about 40 automobiles. They were re-christened the *St. Ignace* and the *Mackinaw City*. The first one started running May 11, 1924, and the other July 24, 1924. During the 1924 season they carried 37,783 cars.

The state highway department estimates that the Straits ferries will this season transport at least 50,000 cars."

-*Northern Michigan Magazine*, August-September, 1926

Postcard message:

Monday 6:00 pm
We are in line waiting for our turn to get on the ferry. Imagine there's 150 cars in line now and we don't leave until 8:30 or so. We are enjoying this trip very much. Certainly some beautiful lakes! Will be at the Soo tomorrow.

-Mabel

Postmarked St. Ignace, 1926
Mailed to Chicago Heights, Ill.

"New Schedule of Ferry Boats
Mackinac Ships Go on Full Summer Count
Each Making Ten Trips

The state automobile ferry service between Mackinaw City and St. Ignace has announced a new schedule which furnishes service between the two points each hour and a half. For July and August the state boats leave each point the following hours: 7:00, 8:30, 10:00, 11:30 a.m. and 1:00, 2:30, 4:00, 5:30, 7:00, 8:30 p.m.

The rate for cars having a wheelbase of up to an including 114 inches is $2.50, and the rate of cars over 114 inches is $3.50. No extra charge for passengers traveling in automobiles, not in excess of the seating capacity of the car. Passengers not traveling in automobiles are charged 25 cents. On trucks, the rate varies from $5 to $15. Autos with trailers are charged an additional $1.50 and motorcycles pay $1 without a sidecar and $1.50 if a sidecar is attached. No package freight other than that carried in automobiles and trucks will be transported.

Two boats are now on the schedule, each vessel having the capacity of about 35 cars. The service is proving very satisfactory to the motorists and a large number cross daily on the State ferries."

-Petoskey Evening News, July 7, 1924

MICHIGAN STATE FERRY

THE STRAITS OF MACKINAC

Mackinaw City, Mich.

New State Ferry
Straits of Mackinac

"The ferry service furnished by the State of Michigan for crossing the Straits of Mackinac received its last augmentation on Wednesday by the arrival of the latest addition to the fleet of ferry steamers built in the past winter and named the *Straits of Mackinac*. The name completes a happily conceived trio of titles involving the two points connected and the narrow stretch of water that breaks the continuity of the trunk line highway, otherwise linking the two parts of the state together…

The *Straits of Mackinac* is much larger than the other two boats; she can carry 60 cars, and presents a fine appearance at dock and out on the lake.

With three boats in service, hourly service will be maintained. The first boat will leave St. Ignace at 6:00 a.m., and from the Mackinaw City side at 6:30 a.m., each to be followed by a boat every hour.

When the height of the season may make it necessary, however, the new ferry will 'run wild,' that is, will unload, load and leave as rapidly as possible without regard to time. In this way she will gain materially on the others as she has a speed of about 15 miles an hour and can make the round trip much faster than can either of the other two."

-*Republican-News,* June 23, 1928

Mackinaw City, Mich.

Postcard message:

Hello Kids:
We are watching the two lakes mix. We drove our car on this boat yesterday
and crossed the Straits. Haven't fished yet. Looks like we ought to get some.
Everywhere is crowded. Will write later.

Marion

Postmarked St. Ignace, 1945
Mailed to Cleveland, Ohio

The *City of Cheboygan*

"Cheboygan, August 12 – The *City of Cheboygan,* Michigan's fourth state-owned automobile ferry, was to be placed in operation at the Straits of Mackinac Sunday, following its christening Saturday at Cheboygan.

The vessel is the largest of the state-owned boats. It is 270 feet long, and has a capacity for 85 or more autos. It will carry cars and passengers between Mackinaw City and St. Ignace, key ports of the lower and Upper Peninsulas. It was formerly the train ferry, *Ann Arbor No. 4,* carrying railroad cars across Lake Michigan. It was purchased by the State Highway department from the Ann Arbor Railroad for $25,000 and remodeled at Cheboygan for $75,000 additional. It was painted white in a manner to conform with the other state ferries.

Other state-owned boats in service at the Straits are the ferries *Mackinaw City, St. Ignace,* and the *Straits of Mackinac.* In addition, the state has leased the auxiliary train ferry *Sainte Marie* as a truck transport, and to carry autos at peak periods; and the state, for rush occasions, also hires the railroad ferry *Chief Wawatam.* However with the ferry traffic increasing over 20 per cent per year, these boats were found to be inadequate, and the state purchased the present steamer, *City of Cheboygan.*

An indication of the need for extra boat service is shown by the fact that during the Fourth of July weekend, autos were lined up for nearly five miles from the Mackinaw City dock waiting an opportunity for transportation across the Straits."

-*Emmet County Graphic,* August 12, 1937

State Car Ferry — City of Munising — Mackinaw City, Mich.

City of Munising in Service

"Escanaba, June 27 – The new Mackinac ferry *City of Munising* steamed toward the Straits today to begin service after being christened amid carnival surroundings at the Escanaba docks. Scheduled to arrive at 1:00 p.m. at St. Ignace, the new craft, built at the Manitowoc, Wis. boat yards, will join four other ferry boats in transferring motorists across the Straits from St. Ignace to Mackinaw City…

The new ferry boat has a capacity of 105 automobiles, greatest of any of the five boats now in service… G. Donald Kennedy, Deputy State Highway Commissioner, pointed out that the present service would be unable to handle the traffic load satisfactorily. He said the only solution was construction of a Straits bridge. A bridge is 'inevitable,' Kennedy said."

-*Cheboygan Daily Tribune*, June 27, 1938.

Mich. State Ferry City of Munising, Mackinaw City, Mich.

Highway on Water

"The Michigan State Highway department ferry fleet which operates year 'round between St. Ignace and Mackinaw City forms a highway on water linking the Upper and Lower Peninsulas of Michigan.

As the traveler takes this restful, 50-minute trip across the Straits of Mackinac aboard comfortable steamers, a scene of rare beauty unfolds before him. The Straits area, the passing steamers and an excellent view of historic and beautiful Mackinac Island make the trip by the state ferry one long to be remembered."

-Michigan State Highway Dept.,
Michigan State Ferry Schedule, Summer 1946

Steamer "Sainte Marie" Plying Straits of Mackinac, Mich.

Increasing Traffic

"The following shows the rapid increase in state ferry traffic at the Straits since 1923:

1923	19,820
1924	38,681
1925	60,332
1926	77,454
1927	90,234
1928	107,566
1929	130,633
1930	132,633
1931	129,858
1932	99,121
1933	107,170
1934	138,302
1935	164,484
1936	206,087
1937	274,749
1938	255,068
1939	280,243
1940	297,000"

-Mackinac Island News,
July 26, 1941

Water Voyage of Thrills and Pleasures

"Crossing the Straits of Mackinac from the Lower Peninsula to the Upper Peninsula of Michigan is an adventure. Some day a bridge may stretch across the tumbling waters wedding these greatly dissimilar sections of the state more closely together, but now the traveler must cross by boat. And in that crossing are packed more thrills and pleasures than ordinarily would be experienced in a water voyage many times longer than the 50-minutes, 9-mile trip from Mackinaw City to Moran Bay, St. Ignace's sheltered harbor, facing the broad sweep of northern Lake Huron.

Six automobile ferries now carry tourists across the Straits. Five are owned by the State Highway Department, and one, the *Sainte Marie*, a railroad car ferry, is chartered by the department. With this fleet of ships moving in a continuous parade back and forth, day and night, in calm and storm, traffic is subject to few long delays except in rush times, such as the hunting season."

-Stace, Arthur, *Touring the Coasts of Michigan,* 1937-1938

The *City of Petoskey*

"The *City of Petoskey* is 338 feet long, 55 feet wide and has a depth of 19 feet, 16 inches. She is 2,775 gross tons. The boat was built in Cleveland in 1901, purchased by the highway department from the Pere Marquette Railway Co. last fall and rebuilt in River Rouge dry dock to serve as an auto ferry. She will carry 120 autos. The boat is propelled by twin screws by a horsepower of 2,500...

Thoroughly reconditioned, the *City of Petoskey*, to be the flagship of the state ferry fleet, is a majestic picture of glistening white. Her quarters are roomy and comfortable. The passenger cabin is commodious and appointed in upholstered chrome furniture of varied color."

-Republican-News and St. Ignace Enterprise, May 29, 1941

Postcard message:

We came across the Straits on this ferry. They sure load them down with big trucks, greyhound buses and cars. Six rows the length of the ship, bumper to bumper. Having a grand rest but will be glad to get home and see all our friends.

- Denny & Florence

Postmarked St. Ignace, 1956
Mailed to Cygnet, Ohio

State Auto Ferry "Vacationland"
Straits of Mackinac

MICHIGAN **STATE FERRY**
SCHEDULES
1954

MICHIGAN STATE HIGHWAY DEPARTMENT
CHARLES M. ZIEGLER — STATE HIGHWAY COMMISSIONER

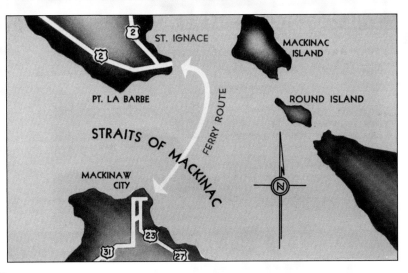

Vacationland to Start Service

"The new $4,500,000 Straits ferry, the *Vacationland,* is set to leave River Rouge tomorrow at 8:00 am, and is due to arrive sometime Friday at the Straits to begin winter ferrying service. The *Vacationland* joins the present fleet of four ships, with 50 per cent more capacity than any one of them, and will handle all winter traffic.

Specially constructed with a heavy steel stiffened hull, it will be the only ice breaker in the fleet. Previously, since 1927, the car ferry, *Ste. Marie,* has been leased from the Mackinaw Transportation Co. for winter run duty.

The new ship, to be the most powerful commercial ship on the Great Lakes, with its four Diesel engines generating 10,000 horse power is 360 feet long and has a beam of 75 feet.

As the ship is constructed the same on each end, called a 'double ender', and is equipped with twin propellers both fore and aft, it will require no turning around for round trip voyages.

This fact, coupled with the new docks located so as to shorten the ferrying distance by two and one half miles per round trip, will increase the fleet capacity by 30 per cent.

The *Vacationland* will carry an average load of 150 vehicles and about 650 passengers. The ferry is equipped with a ship to shore radio telephone, radar, is fireproofed, and can travel 15 miles an hour."

-*Traverse City Record-Eagle,* January 9, 1952

Seasonal Fluctuation

For most of the year the Michigan State Ferry System adequately dealt with the amount of traffic crossing the Straits. The problem was coping with the seasonal fluctuation. Over fifty percent of the traffic came in the summer months. Long lines of cars, trailers, and trucks caused traffic jams on summer holidays and weekends. The ferry service would add extra runs during these times, but had a hard time keeping up with the mass of travelers. The most concentrated traffic jams occurred on the few days preceding the opening of deer season. Delays of ten to fifteen hours, and sometimes longer, were not uncommon. Smart entrepreneurs sold sandwiches, hot coffee, newspapers and other diversions to the cold and hungry folks waiting in line. Running out of gas while waiting was a common occurrence.

State Has Worst Jam in History at Straits

"The biggest traffic jam in Michigan history piled up south of the Straits of Mackinac Saturday as hunters pushed bumper-to-bumper toward the Upper Peninsula for opening of the State's deer hunting season Monday. At 7:00am automobiles were backed up 16 miles on U.S. 27-23 and nine miles on U.S. 31, waiting to be ferried across the Straits between Mackinaw City and St. Ignace. And at 2:00 pm the line still stretched out U.S. 27-23 for 13 miles and out U.S. 31 for seven miles. Enough to stretch three more miles were jammed on the Mackinaw City docks awaiting one of the five state ferries which operated on over-and-back-again schedules. Most of the cars had been in line two to six hours before they got to the docks."

-*Grand Rapids Herald*, November 11, 1954

The Final Voyage

As one era began, another ended. The last car ferry run was made on November 1, 1957, the same day that the Mackinac Bridge was opened to traffic. The 3:00pm final voyage terminated 34 years of operation by the Michigan State Ferry Service. As a final tribute, the dignitaries and press attending the bridge opening ceremonies boarded the *Vacationland* for a last ride to Mackinaw City. A ceremony was held at the St. Ignace dock as Governor Williams and other officials paid their respects to the ferry crews and officers. Souvenir tickets were issued to those dedicated passengers who wanted one last excursion across the waters of the Straits.

Governor G. Mennen Williams inspects a "for sale" sign on one of the state's ferries, the *City of Munising*. The boats, no longer in service, are replaced by the new Mackinac Straits Bridge.

5 Ghost Ships Moored in Sight of Bridge

"MACKINAW CITY, June 25 – Five ghost ships are tied within sight of the proud Mackinac Bridge, sad reminders of the era of steam when they alone linked the two peninsulas of Michigan.

For almost four decades, the state-operated ferry service carried millions of vacationers pursuing happiness in an area where even the air seems different from any place on earth.

Today the immense *Vacationland*, pride of the fleet, is tied up at Mackinaw City. The four others – the *Cities of Cheboygan, Munising, Petoskey* and the *Straits of Mackinac* – are decommissioned at the state docks in St. Ignace. The ships are for sale.

All over the Middle West, people who love the Upper Peninsula have been asking: 'Why can't we have the bridge and the *Vacationland* too?' Letters to every newspaper editor in Michigan have been pointing out that the trip by water has been an important part of a northern holiday. The writers have been demanding that one ferry remain in service to accommodate the thousands who might prefer a leisurely journey on the waters of the Straits…

But under the terms of the indenture covering the bridge bonds, the state agreed not to operate ferries or let anyone else establish a passenger service to compete with the bridge… Every dollar of revenue will be needed to retire the 100 million dollar debt…"

-*Detroit Times*, June 26, 1957

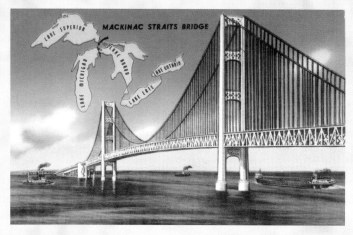

Crossing the Straits — the Mackinac Bridge

The Mackinac Bridge stretches across the five-mile wide Straits of Mackinac from Mackinaw City to St. Ignace. When it was opened for traffic in 1957 the Bridge joined Michigan's two peninsulas with a solid link for the first time since the ice age. As early as 1884 the idea of a "sure and permanent crossing at the Straits" was suggested by the editor of the *Grand Traverse Herald*. When the board of the new Grand Hotel on Mackinac Island met in 1888, Commodore Cornelius Vanderbilt voiced the need for a bridge. The problem of a fixed crossing across the Straits was discussed for many years. Some people favored a tunnel, which was deemed to be too expensive, and others thought a bridge would be a better solution. These early debates planted the germ of an idea that would flourish seven decades later with the building of the Mackinac Bridge.

In 1920 Horatio "Good Roads" Earle, Michigan's first State Highway Commissioner, advocated a submerged floating tunnel. About this same time Charles E. Fowler, a New York engineer, proposed a series of causeways and bridges crossing Lake Huron starting at Cheboygan, then island-hopping for 24 miles to St. Ignace via Bois Blanc, Round and Mackinac Islands. In 1928 the State Highway Department published a report that stated a bridge directly crossing the Straits would cost $30 million, but with the onset of the Depression one year later, no further action was taken.

In 1934 the State Legislature created the Mackinac Straits Bridge Authority to study the feasibility of a bridge. Two plans were presented to the Public Works Administration. A revised island-hopping plan was turned down in 1935 and a direct route plan was denied in 1936. A further step was taken in 1938 when a report was issued that a double-span suspension bridge at the current location was feasible. Work on a causeway from St. Ignace was started in 1941, reaching a mile south into the Straits, however with the onset of World War II all thoughts of a bridge were abandoned. In 1947 the Legislature terminated the Bridge Authority.

In 1948 G. Mennen Williams, a young Navy veteran, ran for Governor of Michigan on the Democratic ticket. Williams promised, if elected, to revive the Mackinac Bridge project. Supporting the new governor's pledge, William Stuart Woodfill, president of the Grand Hotel on Mackinac Island, formed a statewide Mackinac Bridge Citizens Committee in 1949 to lobby for a new bridge authority. Once in office, Williams appointed the Inter-Peninsula Communications Commission to again access the feasibility of building a bridge, taking the bridge study out of the Highway Department. This Commission reported that construction of a bridge across the Straits was possible. In 1950 Governor Williams recommended that a Mackinac Bridge Authority be re-established with the power to build a bridge. Prentiss M. Brown, a former U.S. Senator from St. Ignace and a long proponent of a Straits bridge, headed the seven-man group. Brown was born and raised in St. Ignace and had fought for a bridge during his tenure as senator, even appealing to President Franklin D. Roosevelt. Prentiss M. Brown is known as the "Father of the Mackinac Bridge" for his role in "birthing" the Bridge.

The Commission embraced the idea of building a bridge, but the Legislature denied the group power beyond conducting feasibility studies and determining costs. The Authority hired three bridge experts, including Dr. David B. Steinman, who agreed that a bridge could be built from Mackinaw City to St. Ignace utilizing the causeway already built on the north shore. A bridge was indeed feasible from both engineering and economic standpoints. In 1952 Governor Williams again recommended that the Authority be given power to construct a bridge. The Legislature agreed with the caveat that the bridge be financed by revenue bonds, with no cost to the state and without incurring public debt.

Dr. Steinman, an internationally known bridge engineer, was selected as the chief engineering consultant. Steinman had to overcome many obstacles in his bridge design: the strong winds of the Straits, large ice floes, unpredictable currents, the depths of the waters and the allegedly soft rock deep down under the Straits. Although public enthusiasm was high, there were also skeptics who said a bridge across the Straits could never be built. Steinman proved them wrong with his application of the new science of bridge aerodynamics, which Steinman claimed would make his bridge the "safest large suspension bridge in history." Meanwhile, the process of securing bonds for nearly $100 million dollars was going on. To help sell the bonds the 1953 Legislature agreed that $417,000 per year be diverted from highway funds for operating and maintenance costs of the bridge. This amount was less than the annual deficit suffered by the ferry service. The bonds were to be repaid from toll charges. The original toll for passenger cars, including driver and passengers, was set at $3.25.

By the end of 1953, contracts were signed. The American Bridge Division of United States Steel Corporation of Pittsburgh was awarded the contract to fabricate and erect the steel superstructure. A contract was awarded to the Merritt-Chapman & Scott Corporation of New York to build the concrete and steel foundations. Other contracts were awarded for roadway paving, equipment, administration and service buildings.

The official groundbreaking ceremonies took place on May 7, 1954 on the St. Ignace side and on May 8th on the Mackinaw City side of the Straits. Over the course of the next 42 months, more than 11,500 men were employed on this massive project; 7,500 in quarries, shops and mills; 3,500 at the Bridge site and 350 engineers. The construction was demanding and challenging and had to be meticulous. It could also be hazardous. Five bridge workers lost their lives during the course of construction. Although the work was difficult, it proceeded according to plan and the Bridge opened to traffic on November 1, 1957, exactly the day scheduled four years earlier. There was finally a "sure and permanent crossing" connecting the two peninsulas after 120 years of statehood.

At the time it opened, the Mackinac Bridge was the world's longest suspension span bridge. It was designed to withstand the worst weather conditions that Mother Nature might dish out. The strongest known winds at the Straits reached 78 miles-per-hour, but the Bridge was designed to withstand gale forces of 600 miles-per-hour. The inner lanes on the middle span have an open steel grid surface to allow both wind and snow to flow through. The Bridge was also designed to withstand strong currents and heavy ice pressure. The maximum load equivalent is equal to a continuous line of 50 trucks spaced about 50 feet apart on each of the four lanes.

Thirty-four sub-marine foundations support the long bridge superstructure. The total length of the Bridge, including the approaches, is 26,372 feet, just under five miles. The giant suspension towers, embedded on a rock formation 200 feet below the water's surface, reach 552 feet above the water's surface. The 155-foot clearance under the central suspension span provides enough room for even the largest of the Great Lakes vessels. There are 42,000 miles of suspension cables and almost 6,000,000 bolts and rivets in the structure. The total weight of the Bridge is 1,0024,500 tons. Some 4,000 engineering drawings and 85,000 blueprints were used in construction. The total cost of the Bridge came in at $99,800,000. The four-lane Bridge can handle 6,000 cars an hour as compared with 470 cars per hour on the State car ferries. The crossing takes only ten minutes compared to the 53-minute ferry crossing.

Compared to the structure of other suspension bridges there is little to obstruct the beautiful view. The roadway sits on top of the steel trusses, rather than down within them. The guardrails on each side are below eye level, offering a clear view. For most people, crossing the Bridge for the first time is an awe-inspiring experience, but for others it's a very intimidating task. The Mackinac Bridge Authority offers a Drivers Assistance Program for such timid drivers. Bridge personnel will drive motorcycles, cars and even trucks across the Bridge for those too afraid or nervous to drive themselves. The Bridge reduced mileage between points, providing a shorter travel route for tourists not only visiting Michigan's Upper Peninsula, but those traveling to Wisconsin, Minnesota and other states, as well as Canada.

Although the Bridge was opened to traffic on November 1, 1957, the formal dedication was put off until June of 1958. It was feared that Michigan November weather would be cold and dreary. As it turned out, November 1st was warm and sunny, a perfect Indian Summer day. However, on the first day of the four-day dedication festival, June 26th, the weather was terrible, with blustering winds and dark clouds, much like a typical Michigan November day.

The Mackinac Bridge embodies man's triumph over staggering obstacles and difficulties, both natural and man-made. Steinman viewed the Mackinac Bridge as his masterwork, both a remarkable engineering feat as well as a work of art. As Governor Williams said in 1957, "The Bridge is an expression in steel and concrete, of the will, the determination and the vision of the people of Michigan. It stands as a testimony that no job is too big for the people of this state."

INTERESTING FACTS

Mackinac Bridge Designed by Dr. David B. Steinman

LENGTHS

Total Length of Bridge with Approaches (5 miles)	26,444 Ft.
Total Length Steel Superstructure	19,243 Ft.
Length—Suspension Bridge (Including Anchorages)	8,614 Ft.
Total Length—North Approach Spans	7,129 Ft.
Length—Main Span (Between Main Towers)	3,800 Ft.

HEIGHTS AND DEPTHS

Heights—Main Towers above Water	552 Ft.
Maximum Depth to Rock at Midspan	Unknown
Maximum Depth of Water at Midspan	295 Ft.
Maximum Depth of Tower Piers below Water	210 Ft.

Height of Roadway above Water at Midspan	199 Ft.
Underclearance at Midspan for Ships	155 Ft.
Maximum Depth of Water at Piers	142 Ft.
Maximum Depth of Piers Sunk through Overburden	105 Ft.

CABLES

Total Length of Wire in Main Cables	42,000 Miles
Maximum Tension in Each Cable	16,000 tons
Number Wires in Each Cable	12,580
Weight of Cables	11,840 tons
Diameter of Main Cables	24½ Inches
Diameter of Each Wire	0.196 Inches

MACKINAC BRIDGE

WORLD'S GREATEST BRIDGE

CONNECTING MICHIGAN'S UPPER AND LOWER PENINSULAS AT ST. IGNACE AND MACKINAW CITY.

Michigan Must be United

"A bridge across the Straits of Mackinac will unite the now divided Michigan into one solidified and hence more powerful State. In a stronger union we shall reap increased commercial advantages through the acceleration of freight, mail and passenger travel. Our interlocking financial operations will be stimulated. Transportation time between the extremes and the center of the State will be shortened and a more compact community will be created… The very words, 'Upper' and 'Lower' will lose much of their significance as applied to two peninsulas.

The anticipated benefits so far outweigh all financial and other considerations that everyone, upon due reflection, must conclude that all obstacles to the building of this most needed bridge across the straits must be brushed aside and every effort should be made to hasten completion of the project."

-Michigan Tradesman, October 15, 1941

PROPOSED MACKINAC STRAITS BRIDGE

After years of hope, speculation and frustration the dream of a united Michigan became a reality. Earlier proposals for a bridge across the Straits had all been rejected, but finally the commitment was made and Dr. David B. Steinman was chosen to design the Mackinac Bridge. The internationally famous bridge designer and engineer sought to build a bridge that was structurally sound as well as beautiful, its handsome lines creating a "symphony in steel and stone."

Construction Work

Construction work on the Mackinac Bridge started in May 1954. The largest fleet of construction vessels in the history of bridge building was assembled at the Straits. Over the course of the next 42 months more than 11,500 men were employed on various phases of the construction. The total cost of the project was $99,800,000. The work was painstaking and exacting. Despite formidable difficulties, setbacks with weather and other delays, the construction proceeded according to plan. The Bridge opened to traffic on November 1, 1957, exactly the day scheduled four years earlier.

Foundations clearly show the route the Bridge will take across the Straits.

Two catwalks were laid, from one anchorage to the other so that cables could be spun over the towers.

Iron workers secure stiffening truss out from south tower.

Construction crews continue their work into the night, spinning cable across the main span.

Year-By-Year Timetable for the Bridge

"David B. Steinman, of New York, consulting engineer for the Mackinac Bridge project, lists the following schedule for construction work:

1954 – Mobilization of equipment; start construction of north anchorage; fabrication of caissons for main tower piers and six piers for south truss spans; construction of 12 truss span piers between north anchorage and St. Ignace causeway.

1955 – Construction of main tower and cable bent piers; start construction on south anchorage; erection of main towers, cable bents and 12 north truss spans.

1956 – Complete tower erection; spinning of suspension cables; construction of south truss span piers and erection of 16 truss spans between Mackinaw City shore and south anchorage; construction of Mackinaw City approach.

1957 – Construction of northern approach over St. Ignace causeway with roadway to be elevated to 30 feet above water level; completion of both anchorages; completion of cable suspender erection; erection of suspended spans; paving of two outer roadway lanes; construction of northern approach to St. Ignace causeway; completion of toll booths, administration and maintenance buildings and equipment.

Wrapping the main cables and painting the bridge will proceed in 1958 after the structure is open to traffic."

-Baird, Willard, *Modern Miracle: a Series of Articles Concerning the Mackinac Straits Bridge*, 1952.

A tug pulls a pre-constructed section of truss out into the Straits, where it will be lifted high above the surface to become part of the bridge.

3,700 tons of reinforcing steel were used to build the structure supporting the roadbed.

Great Tourist Wonder

"Visitors to the eastern gateway to 'Hiawatha Land' will see under construction what will become one of the world's man-made wonders, the Straits of Mackinac Bridge. This great span, which will stretch five miles from Highway US-2 at St. Ignace to Highway US-31 at Mackinaw City, will connect Michigan's two Peninsulas. It is scheduled for completion late in 1957.

For years, Upper Peninsula residents dreamed, hoped, prayed and worked for a span across the Straits... Now, they're eagerly awaiting the day when they can drive across the $99,000,000 structure. Undoubtedly it will be one of the great tourist wonders of the Midwest."

-Upper Peninsula Development Bureau, *The Lure of Michigan's Upper Peninsula,* 1955

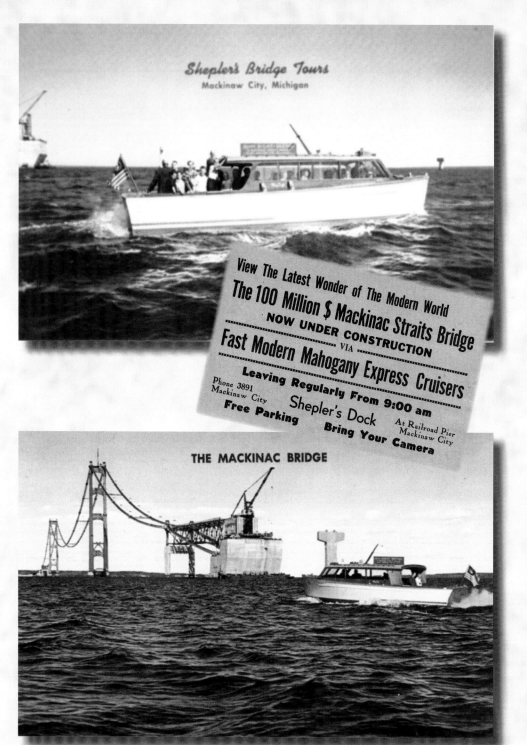

Shepler's Bridge Tours
Mackinaw City, Michigan

View The Latest Wonder of The Modern World
The 100 Million $ Mackinac Straits Bridge
NOW UNDER CONSTRUCTION
VIA
Fast Modern Mahogany Express Cruisers
Leaving Regularly From 9:00 am
Phone 3891
Mackinaw City
Shepler's Dock   At Railroad Pier
Mackinaw City
Free Parking   Bring Your Camera

THE MACKINAC BRIDGE

Postcard message:

Dear Trent:
Well I took off for the north woods for a week to cool off but it is hot here too. We took a boat trip tonight to see the new bridge work. There is a lot of stuff out there already,

Love, Frances

Postmarked Saint Ignace, 1956
Mailed to Muskegon, Mich.

"Boat for 'Rubber-neckers'

Bill Shepler has the answer to a question that's voiced by hundreds of tourists visiting the Straits of Mackinac who always ask: 'How can we get close to see the big bridge?' Bill operates a 'rubber-neck' boat… Those who seek him out get a ringside seat to the big show – the construction of the Mackinac Straits bridge.

This is his third season of taking sightseers into the Straits to watch, and he thinks his new enterprise is just beginning to flourish. 'After the bridge is finished,' he said, 'there will be more boating activity and more sightseeing than ever before.'

Before construction of the big bridge started Bill operated a busy water taxi business ferrying customers to Mackinac Island. He still keeps one boat for that run, but his professional pride now centers on the big 34-foot, twin-screw cruiser that he built just for the rubberneck trade.

After two full seasons of ferrying sightseers, Bill thinks tourists have a uniform curiosity. 'They all have the same four questions to ask,' he said. 'They want to know how long it will be, how high it is, how deep the water is and when will it be done.'

To keep a jump or two ahead of eager question askers, Bill has developed a little 'patter' he delivers as soon as the cruiser is comfortably away from the dock.

It starts like this: 'Folks you're about to see the eighth wonder of the world, the Mackinac Straits bridge, five and one-half miles long, 552 feet high…'

While Bill handles the bridge traffic from the southern approach to the big span, a similar service is offered for tourists approaching from the north. At St. Ignace the Arnold Transit Co. line also operates a bridge sightseeing service."

-Grand Rapids Press, July 2, 1956

The Dream Emerges

The Bridge under construction was a sight to see from the waters of the Straits. During the course of construction, Bridge sightseeing was a popular attraction for convention goers and various tour groups. The Michigan bankers convention held on Mackinac Island in June of 1956 chartered one of the Arnold Transit Company's boats to view "what was beginning to look like a bridge." A year later the Grand Rapids Chamber of Commerce chartered the *S.S. North American* and saw amazing progress. The Bridge was visible from about 20 miles away as the boat sailed up to the Straits. The towers appeared "as slender as matchsticks" sticking up on the horizon. As the boat got within five or six miles the cables and approach stands came into view. Then the "erector set impression" of the $100 million Bridge evaporated and the structure could be envisioned as a bona fide bridge linking the two peninsulas. The dream emerged as a reality.

The Grand Rapids Chamber of Commerce Good Fellowship Cruise in June of 1957 had a close-up view of the Bridge construction from the deck of the *S.S. North American.*

Governor Williams Pays First Toll Fee

"The mighty Mackinac Bridge linking Michigan's two peninsulas with bonds of steel and concrete was opened to traffic today. The official opening was climaxed this afternoon when Gov. G. Mennen Williams, making the first 'official' crossing, motored from Mackinaw City to St Ignace where he paid the first $3.25 toll collected on the 100 million dollar span. William's toll payment was meant to dramatize the fact that nobody, not even the governor, will get free passage until the five-mile span is paid for. The Bridge, whose completion spelled an end for the state car ferry fleet plying the Straits of Mackinac between Lakes Michigan and Huron, also was hailed as Michigan's biggest historical event in 100 years…

Immediately after Williams and other members of the official party made their initial crossing, vehicles lined up for a mile on both sides of the Straits swarmed onto the new span. The official opening was preceded by an inspection tour during which a motorcade of 300 dignitaries in 65 cars and four buses rolled out onto the Bridge shortly before noon. Williams and other dignitaries making an official inspection party motored onto the Bridge at 11:10 a.m. as the northern Water Wonderland provided some of its best fall weather… Williams, members of the Mackinac Bridge Authority and the Ontario Highway Minister posed for pictures and expressed their pleasure in making the first official tour of the span."

-*Holland Evening Sentinel,* November 1, 1957

Mackinac Bridge Opens to Traffic

The Mackinac Bridge was opened for traffic on November 1, 1957, just in time for deer hunting season. Thousands of people thronged St. Ignace and Mackinaw City to be part of this historic occasion. Some were locals who had watched the construction for the past four years. Others traveled hundreds of miles just to be one of the first motorists to cross the Bridge that skeptics said could never be built. More than 200 leaders of industry, finance, government and labor were on hand. Governor G. Mennen Williams, in his signature bow tie, headed the official inspection party. About 50 members of both the House and Senate of the Michigan Legislature accepted invitations for the ceremony. Prentiss M. Brown and others members of the Mackinac Bridge Authority attended the day's festivities. Dr. David B. Steinman, designer and chief engineer of the Bridge, flew in from New York. Over 100 photographers and scores of reporters were on hand to document the event. Area schools closed for the day. Speeches were made, flags and banners waved, freighters blasted their whistles and vendors sold souvenirs of this day to be long remembered.

Hundreds of cars lined up on both the St. Ignace and Mackinaw City sides of the Straits waiting to cross. The Mackinac Bridge Authority issued cards certifying that one had crossed the new Bridge on the first day it was open for traffic.

STATE OF MICHIGAN

MACKINAC BRIDGE AUTHORITY

THIS IS TO CERTIFY THAT

Donald L. Geske, Sr.

CROSSED THE MACKINAC BRIDGE ON NOV. 1, 1957, THE FIRST DAY IT WAS OPEN FOR TRAFFIC.

Prentiss M Brown

Chairman Mackinac Bridge Authority

MACKINAC BRIDGE DEDICATION FESTIVAL
THURSDAY   FRIDAY   SATURDAY   JUNE   26   -   28   1958

Mackinac Bridge Dedication Festival
June 26, 27, 28, 1958

A tremendous amount of planning went into the dedication festival. Everything was thoroughly arranged, down to the donuts offered to the press corps. Events were planned for St. Ignace, Mackinaw City, Cheboygan, Sault Ste. Marie, Harbor Springs and Petoskey. Although the Bridge was opened to traffic on November 1, 1957, the formal dedication was delayed until June of 1958, since the weather in June was usually much nicer than Michigan's November weather. As it turned out, however, November 1st was a beautiful sunny day in the 60s, while the first day of the June festival was cold and raining with blustering winds.

Thursday, June 26th was "St. Ignace Day." There were exhibits set up at the State ferry docks with civic, governmental, industrial, boating and military displays, including open houses on U.S. Naval and Coast Guard ships in dock. The first big parade, a two-mile procession with floats and marching bands, marched through St. Ignace, with jets flying over the parade route. Evening festivities included a play, a searchlight display and fireworks.

Many of the same events were repeated on Friday, which was "Mackinaw City Day." There was another parade with celebrities, floats, horsemen, and military personnel. A reenactment of Jean Nicolet's 1634 passage through the Straits was performed in a birch bark canoe. A historical marker was dedicated at old Fort Michilimackinac. The Friday evening celebration included a military band concert, followed by square dancing and more fireworks.

Saturday was the culmination of the festival and the weather cleared in time for the formal dedication of the Bridge. Access to the Bridge ceremonies was by invitation only. The public could hear the proceedings at the exhibit areas on both sides of the Bridge over a public address system. A ribbon tying, rather than a ribbon cutting, ceremony took place followed by a prayer. Prentiss M. Brown, chairman of the Mackinac Bridge Authority, was master of ceremonies. Speeches were given by various dignitaries, including Governor G. Mennen Williams, who said "Today, we the people of Michigan, give this Bridge to America." Army Secretary Wilbur Bruckner read a telegram from President Eisenhower calling the Bridge a "combination of the vision, confidence and daring of free men working together…of far reaching economic benefits of the state and nation." Dr. David Steinman, designer of the Bridge, described the Bridge as "the highest achievement of art and science." Low flying jets thundered over the Bridge and punctuated the ceremony with their roars. Passing freighters sounded whistles in salutes.

A Procession of 83 Beauty Queens

A motorcade of beauty queens from each of Michigan's 83 counties traveled across the Bridge on Friday, June 27, 1958 from St. Ignace to Mackinaw City. The young women returned on Saturday to participate in the dedication ceremonies. Six miles of green satin ribbon, four inches wide, were strung to the 1958 Oldsmobile convertibles of the 83 beauties. The caravan of Upper Peninsula queens left from St. Ignace, while the procession of the Lower Peninsula queens left from Mackinaw City. Meeting at the north anchor block, the ribbons were ceremoniously tied together by Governor and Mrs. G. Mennen Williams and Mr. and Mrs. Prentiss Brown. About 1,000 people cheered as the ribbons were knotted. The tied ribbon symbolized the linking of Michigan's two peninsulas and formally dedicated the Mighty Mac.

Commemorative Stamps

"Weary postal workers at St. Ignace and Mackinaw City heaved a collective sigh of relief Thursday after passing their biggest test. Together, they put out more than 450,000 first-day 'covers' of the new 3-cent stamp commemorating the Mackinac Bridge. The blueish-green stamp went on sale for the first time Wednesday, June 25, at the two terminal cities at the bridge. They are now available in all the nearly 37,000 post offices across the country.

Stamp collectors from throughout the nation and foreign lands as well flooded the local post offices with requests for first-day cancellations… The stamp was a special prize for at least two reasons. It was the first to carry the name of a bridge for a postmark and the last 3-cent commemorative to be issued before the cost of a first-class letter goes up to 4-cents Aug. 1."

-*Grand Rapids Herald*, June 27, 1958

Mackinac Bridge Walk

The first Mackinac Bridge Walk took place on June 25, 1958 as part of the dedication festival and was sponsored by the International Walkers Association. Over 100 people led by Governor G. Mennen Williams sloshed the five miles across the Bridge in rain and heavy fog. Each walker had to pre-qualify the day before by doing a practice walk across the Bridge to make sure that he or she could make the long haul.

The 1958 Bridge walk spurred an interest in making it a yearly event. The second annual Bridge walk took place on Labor Day in 1959. The idea was popular since the Bridge was closed to pedestrian traffic at all other times. For the first several years the direction of the walkers alternated between northbound and southbound. Men, women and children of all ages participated in the event and by 1964 the number of walkers soared to 6,000. It was decided that future walks would progress southbound. Most of the walkers were from the Lower Peninsula and wanted to return to their vehicles as quickly as possible when their walk ended. In previous years these walkers had to wait for bus transportation at St. Ignace to return to Mackinaw City.

The Labor Day Bridge Walk was billed as the "world's greatest walking event" and drew professional racers and celebrities as well as ordinary folk. In 1966 Governor George Romney was the first governor to walk the Bridge since former Governor G. Mennen Williams inaugurated the event. Many other governors of Michigan have since hiked the five-mile span. In election years it is a common practice for all breeds of politicians to walk the Bridge and take advantage of the photo-ops it provides. Many other Michigan communities have started their own Labor Day "bridge walks" across local bridges of much less magnitude.

Governor G. Mennen Williams stands with the oldest and youngest walkers to complete the first Bridge walk: 87 year-old Joe Barnette of Cincinnati and 4 year-old Daniel Geske of Grand Rapids. To the right of Daniel are his brother Donald and their mother Louise Geske.

Tolls

The toll plaza was constructed on the St. Ignace side of the Bridge. When the Bridge opened in 1957 the toll was set at $3.25 for each passenger automobile, but there was no extra charge for the driver or passengers. The ferry rate had been $2.75 for passenger cars, plus an extra 25 cents for the driver and each passenger. The ferry service had charged trucks according the their length, but on the Bridge, weight was the more important factor. Not wanting to use a scale system, a formula was created relating weight to the number of axles to determine toll fees for trucks. The Mackinac Bridge Authority needed to collect revenue to repay the bond issues, but also didn't want the toll to be significantly higher than the ferry rates that travelers were accustomed to paying.

New Experience in Highway Travel

"The magnificent Mackinc Bridge, connecting Michigan's two peninsulas, is one of the great bridges of the world...it not only offers tourists an exciting new experience in highway travel, it expedites commerce and unites the State with a bond of permanence and beauty...The fast growing network of expressways and the Mackinac Bridge will give Michigan a modern highway system second to none in America."

-Michigan State Highway Department, *Michigan Official Highway Map*, 1958

A Proud Symbol

The Mackinac Bridge quickly became a proud symbol of the State of Michigan, but it also grew into a commercial tool and was used to advertise everything from Portland cement to Pontiac automobiles. To commemorate the official dedication of the Mackinac Bridge, Leonard Service Stations offered a free souvenir frosted tumbler with the purchase of ten gallons or more of Leonard gasoline. There was even a "Big Mac" beer brewed by the Menominee-Marinette Brewing Co.

Postcard message:

Crossed the bridge in sunlight today with the bottom of a rainbow to the East. Tonight had supper at St. Ignace and had a grand look at the bridge with lights from high ground over there.
- Lucille, Arlene, Gertrude & Jane

Postmarked Mackinaw City, 1958
Mailed to Kalamazoo, Mich.

Eighth Wonder of the World

Motels, restaurants, gas stations and souvenir shops started dotting the Straits region's landscape in the 1950s as more people traveled to the area for vacation. When the Bridge opened even larger flocks of tourists came to see the "Eighth Wonder of the World." There was an enormous boom in the development of facilities and services to serve the needs of the large influx of visitors. Accommodations with Bridge views commanded top rates and restaurants printed images of the Bridge on their placemats. All sorts of businesses looked for ways to cash in on the popularity of the new Bridge. A wide array of Mackinac Bridge souvenirs appeared on the scene when the Bridge opened. These included pennants, pins, windshield decals, ashtrays, playing cards, letter openers, shoe horns, aprons, scarves, plates, trays, glass tumblers, towels, lighters, T-shirts, compacts and, of course, postcards.

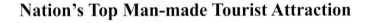

Nation's Top Man-made Tourist Attraction

Tourist leaders predicted that the Mackinac Bridge would become the nation's top man-made tourist attraction and a magnet for tourist dollars. Tourists not only came to view the new Bridge, they now could cross the Straits in a matter of ten minutes. Many of these bridge-gazers would not have otherwise journeyed into the Upper Peninsula, but with the easy crossing they heeded the call of adventure. Recreational opportunities opened in Michigan's U. P., which could now be reached in a day's drive from many of the cities in the Midwest. The Upper Peninsula Development Bureau believed that the Bridge would open up a new era rich with opportunities for the people of the U.P. and benefit the entire state. Local businesses, and chambers of commerce, as well as the state's tourist associations actively promoted Michigan's "new scenic wonder...the longest single-span suspension bridge in the world." Although it can no longer make that claim, tourists and travelers today still marvel at the majesty and magnitude of the Mighty Mac.

Chapter Four – St. Ignace

St. Ignace is the southernmost settlement in the Eastern Upper Peninsula, jutting into the Straits of Mackinac. Its beautiful hillside setting overlooks a natural harbor. It is the second oldest settlement in Michigan and its name honors Father (Pere) Marquette of St. Ignatius Loyola, the founder of the Jesuits.

Jean Nicolet first sighted St. Ignace Point in 1634 while pushing westward through the Straits, seeking a northwest passage to China. In 1671 Pere Marquette, the French explorer and missionary, established a mission at St. Ignace. It was from this point two years later that the French priest and his fellow explorer, Louis Jolliet, set out on their journey to discover the "Father of Waters," the Mississippi River. The mission at St. Ignace was abandoned in 1706 and burned by the priests to prevent its desecration. This mission was renewed and visited by the French missionary and explorer, Pierre Francois Xavier de Charlevoix in 1721.

Pere Marquette died in 1675 at the mouth of the Pere Marquette River near Ludington and was buried there by his Native American companions. Honoring his wish to return to "his little chapel at the Straits," his Native American friends returned two years later and reburied his remains underneath the floor of the log chapel at St. Ignace. After the mission church was burned in 1706, the location of Marquette's grave was unknown until it was identified in 1877. The citizens of St Ignace marked the grave with a simple granite shaft which stands in Marquette Park.

The French built Fort DeBaude at St. Ignace about 1680, not too long after Marquette's mission was founded. The fort was named to honor Count Frontenac, Canada's Governor General (Baude was his family name). When Frontenac lost favor, the fort was renamed Fort Michilimackinac. It was the first French fort in the Upper Great Lakes region and was occupied for about two decades. A garrison of 200 soldiers served under various military leaders, including Antoine de la Mothe Cadillac. Cadillac left to take command of a new fort in Detroit in 1701. Most of the garrison and many Native Americans went with him. This first Fort Michilimackinac was succeeded in 1715 by another fort of the same name on the south shore of the Straits, in the location of today's Mackinaw City.

For the next 100 years, St. Ignace continued with a few residents, mostly fur traders and Native Americans. In the early part of the 19th century, fishermen from Canada settled in the St. Ignace area and developed a steady fishing trade in whitefish and Mackinaw trout. The settlement started to grow and a dock was built in 1872. About this same time the lumbering industry started to take hold. For the next few decades fishing and lumbering were the main economic interests of St. Ignace.

In 1881, the Detroit, Mackinac & Marquette Railroad (later the Duluth, South Shore & Atlantic) connected St. Ignace with Duluth. That same year a railroad car ferry across the Straits ended St. Ignace's years of isolation from the Lower Peninsula. The rail connection made St. Ignace into a viable lumber port. A strong freight transfer business developed, shifting freight from boats and trains. The county seat moved from Mackinac Island to St. Ignace in 1882. That same year St. Ignace was incorporated as a village, and a year later, was incorporated as a city.

As the natural resources of fur, timber and fish dwindled, St. Ignace started developing a tourist trade. Hotels that had earlier served the railroad trade now started to attract a new tourist clientele. By 1881, four hotels operated in the village: the Northern House, the Union House, the Lake View House, and the Marquette House. More hotels, including the Dunham House, Central Hotel and several others, were built as the steamship lines brought more visitors to the city.

Two factors were important in developing tourism in the 1920s, promotion of the area and the car ferry service. Clarence C. Eby was a pioneer in the region's tourism industry and souvenir trade. For several years, starting in 1923, he published a visitor's guide, entitled *Mackinac County of the Straits Country*. Over the years he owned several of the area's top tourist attractions, including Indian Village, Castle Rock and Curio Fair. St. Ignace got a boost in 1923 when ferry service was established across the Straits; the service became the city's largest employer. The ferries brought thousands of visitors to St. Ignace each summer and local businesses prospered from the tourist trade.

Vacationers were drawn to the area for its pleasing scenery, pleasant summers and recreational opportunities. Fishing, hunting, boating, swimming and golf were popular activities. The landscape became dotted with summer homes and rental cottages. The Straits State Park was opened in 1924. For some travelers St. Ignace was a stop on their way to further places in the Upper Peninsula. Others stayed in the area, making short trips to Mackinac Island, the Les Cheneaux Islands, or other points of interest. When the Mackinac Bridge opened in 1957, even more tourists discovered the charms of St. Ignace. Today it joins Mackinaw City to form a tourist hub for northern Michigan.

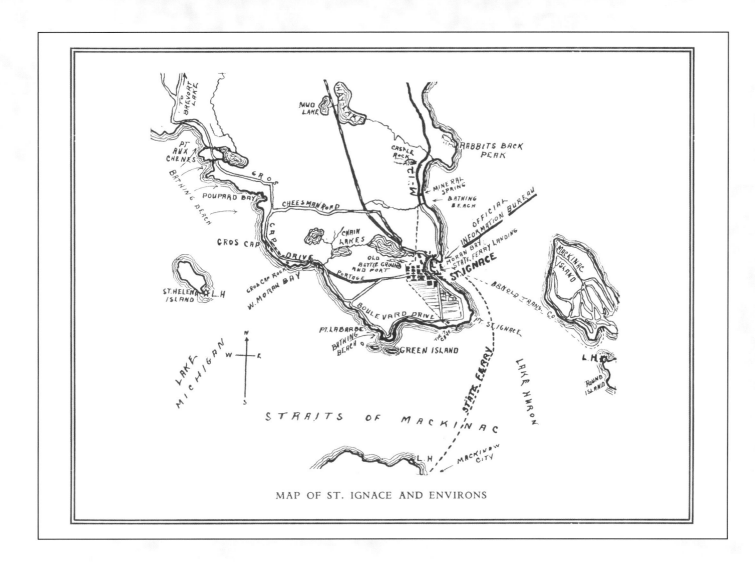

MAP OF ST. IGNACE AND ENVIRONS

St. Ignace

"St. Ignace has a fine natural harbor. It is easily reached by rail, water or air, and offers good shipping facilities, low power rates and cheap lands. Excellent modern hotels, cottage and garage accommodations are offered at moderate rates. Besides one of the finest state camp sites in Michigan. St. Ignace has several private tourist camps and camp cottage accommodations… St. Ignace is located in a land of evergreen, where pine, balsam and cedar fill the air with their healing and exhilarating perfume. Thousands afflicted with hay fever find virtually immediate relief. The visitor in St. Ignace will find attractions which will keep him interested for a long, delightful period. There are wonderful side trips for those who make this their vacation headquarters."

-Upper Michigan Ahoy Vacationist, circa 1930

Connecting Point for Transportation

"The natural situation of St. Ignace, the judicial seat of Mackinac County, offers exceptional advantages for manufacturing, for commerce and for summer resort purposes… St. Ignace has a deep, wide and safe harbor, one of the best on the lakes. The shipping of the Great Lakes between Chicago and Buffalo, Detroit and Duluth, traverses her adjacent waters. The huge car ferries *St. Ignace* and *Ste. Marie* make four to eight trips daily across the Straits of Mackinac…and

these powerful boats keep the channel open all winter, thus connecting this point with the Michigan Central R.R. and the Grand Rapids & Indiana R.R. at Mackinaw City and in effect, extending those roads to St. Ignace. During the summer, the Detroit & Mackinac R.R., which at present has its northern terminus at Cheboygan, is connected with St. Ignace by a double daily steamer service. Excellent transportation service by water is maintained between this place and all other Great Lakes points. The Detroit & Cleveland steamers, which make St. Ignace their northern terminus, and which call here daily, offer to passengers, as well as for freight, unexcelled service from Detroit, Toledo, Cleveland, Buffalo and other Lake Huron and Lake Erie points. The *Illinois* and *Missouri* call here, as well as the Lake Michigan & Lake Superior Transportation Company's steamers on their way from Chicago to Duluth, and from Green Bay and way ports we have the Hart line. Passengers arriving on steamers, which include Mackinac Island their only port of call in this vicinity, are transferred without loss of time by local steamers constantly plying between the island and St. Ignace."

-Polk, R. L. & Co., *Michigan Gazetteer*, 1911

Postcard message:

June 12, 1912
Wednesday morning
Am now waiting for the steamer for Mackinac Island. Leaves at 8:15a.m. A good steady wind blowing and a heavy sea and good November weather —Ha Ha. Great place this is.   F.

Postmarked Saint Ignace, 1912
Mailed to Salem, Mass

THE BEACH AT, — GRAHAM'S POINT, — ST. IGNACE, MICH.

A Summer Resort

"As a summer resort St. Ignace combines the natural attractions of all other summer resorts. She is picturesquely enthroned in the midst of a country that is perpetual delight. Her atmosphere is a tonic to tired nerves and sure death to hay fever. Every inhalation adds vigor to the body and length to life. A feeling of physical uplift and exhilaration takes possession of the sojourner, to his permanent benefit. The great waters that kiss her shores – Lake Michigan, Lake Huron, Moran Bay and the Straits of Mackinac – extend a continual invitation to those who love boating and fishing. In these and in the woodland lakes and trout streams, hidden in the nearby forests, perch, black bass, pike, pickerel, Mackinaw trout and brook trout are waiting to try conclusions with any willing rod-wielder. For those who would rather loaf and dream, there are woody walks, pebbly beaches, stretches of blue water, romantic woods and beautiful drives, and there are no mosquitoes or noxious insects to share your slumbers, your reveries or your rambles and bring you back to the unpleasant realization that you are still on earth and not in Elysium."

-Polk, R. L. & Co., *Michigan Gazetteer,* 1907

A City of Modern Improvements

"Today St. Ignace is a city of modern improvements. It has fine, broad cement walks, good streets, electric lights, the purest of water, a bank and two newspapers. Its hotels and boarding houses offer excellent service and the prices are proportioned to the services rendered, but in no case exorbitant. They treat you right and do not rob you."

Polk, R. L. & Co., *Michigan Gazetteer,* 1907

BIRD'S-EYE VIEW OF ST. IGNACE, MICH.

FATHER MARQUETTE'S MONUMENT
AND PARK
ST. IGNACE, MICH.

Postcard message:

Dear Friends,
We have been spending our vacation days in the Upper Pen. This
a.m. we were on the very top of this rock. There is a viewing
platform on top. The rock looks very much like a face or skull.
We are now on the boat going home and about to anchor at
Cheboygan. We want to hear from you as soon as the large bird
makes you a visit.

-Monroe & Lillian

Postmarked Cheboygan, 1914
Mailed to Topeka, Kansas

ST. ANTHONY ROCK, ST. IGNACE, MICH.

Fascinating History

"While Upper Michigan is replete with landmarks of a fascinating early history, perhaps no other district enjoys as much of that atmosphere as Mackinac County. Here, at St. Ignace, the county seat, is found the grave of Father Marquette, the 'Guardian Angel of the Ottawa Mission.'

In 1671 Father Marquette, intrepid explorer and missionary, established a mission at St. Ignace, and it was from this point two years later that the good father, with his brother explorer, Joliet, set out upon their journey to discover the 'Father of Waters'.

As you stand there in Marquette Park, gazing at the tall, granite spire which marks the grave of Father Marquette, you are awed by its solemnity and significance. In fact the hills which bound old St. Ignace to the north, east and west, are likewise rich in Indian lore – for the thrilling details of many an early struggle are buried deep beneath their sod."

-Upper Peninsula Development Bureau, *Cloverland: The Tourist's Paradise*, circa 1930

Rabbit's Back Point

"Visit Rabbit's Back Point. Here one may find Pedestal Rock, Devil's Chair, Kingfisher Rock, Hiawatha's Thumb, The Pebbles, domes of the old French lime kilns and a pleasing bit of beach dotted here and there with fishermen's shacks and net racks, as well as Echo Cleft and Porcupine Cave, which is said to be the hiding place of hunted men of the dim past. The view from the peak, known to Red Men as Wa-bas-o Ma-da-bin (rabbit sitting down) unfolds a breathtaking panorama of the Straits Country."

-Eby, C.C., *Mackinac County of the Straits Country,* circa 1925

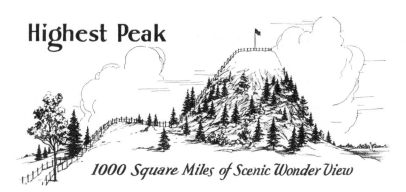

RABBIT'S BACK PEAK, ST. IGNACE, MICHIGAN

Pleasing Accommodations

"The claims of St. Ignace as a summer resort fully equal, and in some points excel, those of the celebrated Mackinac Island; and, in truth, the visitor may enjoy all the charms of the latter without several of the disadvantages accompanying an actual residence there… The people of St. Ignace, alive to the beauties and attractions of their city, add to her advantages by making it possible for the tourist of moderate means, who cannot afford the luxury of visiting the highly expensive watering places, to come here for his summer outing; to enjoy his holiday most thoroughly and to obtain hotel or boarding house accommodations at surprisingly low rates. St. Ignace is in the center of the Mackinac tourist district…"

- City of St. Ignace and Mackinac County, for the Year 1895

Postcard message:

Dear Friend,
Have just had a breakfast of coffee, toast & egg which costs a quarter. Had a lovely trip as I took a boat from Chicago up here & I don't care if I ever go back to work or not. But I will soon have to. The water and boats – all the best scenery.
Sincerely, Thelma

Postmarked Saint Ignace, 1908
Mailed to Topeka, Kansas

Dunham House

"This extremely popular house is owned and conducted by James M. Campbell, and can accommodate fifty guests. To those who desire to reside for a period in this city, and who are seeking a quiet and homelike place of abode, we can especially recommend the Dunham House, as there is no bar or saloon in connection with it to make matters unpleasant to those who do not care for this feature of hotel life. This house has a reputation of setting an excellent table with a pleasing variety of food, well cooked and tastefully served and nothing is lacking that first-class management can suggest to add to the comfort and convenience of the guests… The rates are reasonable, being $1.50 daily and special weekly arrangements being made with continuous boarders."

-City of St. Ignace and Mackinac County, for the Year 1895

HOTEL NORTHERN ❦ WELCH, McINTYRE & WELCH

European—Service a la Carte

MODERNLY EQUIPPED.—204-FOOT LOBBY AND DINING ROOMS OVERLOOKING THE
STRAITS OF MACKINAC.—RECREATION HALL IN CONNECTION

100 Guest Rooms—50 with Private Bath.   Weekly Rates Arranged.   Phone 19.   ST. IGNACE, MICH.

Attention to Travelers

Before the days of the big national hotel chains, small hotels and family-owned lodges and resorts often paid special attention to their guests, knowing that a satisfied customer was likely to return. Many of these establishments advertised their home-like surroundings and family atmosphere. Some offered weary travelers home-cooked meals. Families who ran these hotels and resorts had to be versatile, cooking pancakes, washing sheets, repairing the roof and doing a hundred other tasks all in a day's work.

EVERGREEN LODGE
St. Ignace, Michigan

EVERGREEN LODGE
St. Ignace, Michigan

Postcard message:

July 1st, 8pm
Dear Mother & Dad,
Got as far as Duck Creek Sunday night – a few miles out of
Green Bay. Left Green Bay at eight this morning and arrived
here about 5:30pm. We'll stay here for at least two days.
Beautiful place, everything OK.

-Love, Art & Loretta

Postmarked Saint Ignace, 1940
Mailed to Forest Park, Ill.

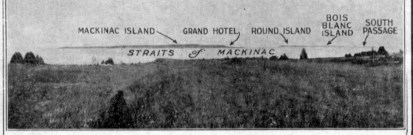
Summer Cottages

Summer cottages began dotting the landscape around St. Ignace in the 1920s and 1930s. The Gateway City Improvement Company promoted cottage development with "lots and bungalows for sale and cottages built to order." People who had vacationed in the area were drawn to building their own summer homes. Some also built mom-and-pop cabins to rent. The income supported their dream of a summer spent in the Straits region, away from the hectic life of the city. Cottagers fell in love with the scenery, the lakes and beaches, the fishing and hunting opportunities and the invigorating climate of the St. Ignace area.

A Cottage Movement

"A movement has already started which apparently will not end until our shores in all directions are dotted with cottages. Those who have spent some time here during past seasons are now enthusiastic boosters for the cottage movement and many lots have been sold for the erection of summer homes."

-Eby, C.C., *Mackinac County of the Straits Country,* circa 1924

Cabin Courts, Motor Courts and Motels

The mom-and-pop cabins of the 1930s and 1940s gradually evolved into "cabin courts" and "motor courts." These establishments were usually located on a main highway and welcomed guests staying for just a night or two. By the 1950s motels, as we know them today, were dotting the landscape of the St. Ignace area. Their number increased dramatically with the opening of the Mackinac Bridge. These St. Ignace lodgings were often the jumping-off point for travelers on their trips to explore the marvels of the Upper Peninsula.

Miles' Cabins
ST. IGNACE, MICHIGAN
Hiawathaland's
Finest Cabin Court
Higgins Boats · DISTRIBUTORS OF · Alma Trailers

MAPLE REST CABINS ST. IGNACE, MICH. L-1634

Postcard message:

Wed. eve.
Dear Dad,
We are at a grand tourist camp here at St. Ignace. 2 bedrooms, kitchen, shower bath, and everything – just like home. We had a real home-cooked meal tonight – and all for $4.00. I think we are going towards Houghton Lake tomorrow.
Love, Ginny

Postmarked Saint Ignace, date not legible
Mailed to Litchfield, Mich.

MILES' CABIN COURT AND TRAILER PARK
ST. IGNACE, MICH.

21035

Island View Cabins

ISLAND VIEW LODGE 39 LOG CABINS ST. IGNACE, MICH.
L-1605

"Our cabins are different from the majority seen on the highway. Located in St. Ignace, on Highway 31, just one and one-quarter miles from downtown is your vacation home, where you and your family and friends may stop after the day's touring and enjoy 'the REST of your life' in clean, cozy and economical Log Cabins. These cabins are recommended and approved by all the Auto Clubs in the middle west and by the State Health Department of Michigan… While here you are constantly breathing that evergreen fragrance so much desired for your rest, health and happiness… Use these cabins as your headquarters while vacationing and from them make those delightful, daily trips, where you are always viewing something different and unusual."

-Island View Cabins, circa 1945

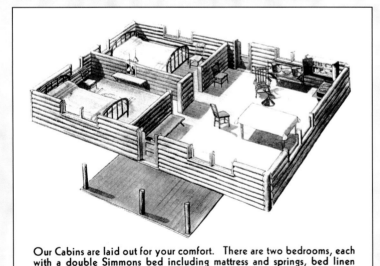

Our Cabins are laid out for your comfort. There are two bedrooms, each with a double Simmons bed including mattress and springs, bed linen and blankets. The living room has a cook stove with a pile of wood beside it, cooking utensils and dishes, knives, forks and spoons. Electricity is in every Cabin.

ISLAND VIEW CABINS
ST. IGNACE - MICHIGAN
ON THE STRAITS OF MACKINAC.

for the 'REST' of your life

COMPLETELY FURNISHED-
COZY, COMFORTABLE, CLEAN

daily or weekly rates.

Postcard Message:

This makes a nice honeymoon retreat, don't you think? that's just what it is, was married last week Monday. Will write you when we return to Detroit. Am very happy and I know you're going to like him. He likes you already.

Love, Kit

Postmarked St. Ignace, 1953
Mailed to Schenectady, N.Y.

Birchwood Opening Drew Crowds Tuesday

"By tremendous effort Ellsworth Vallier had his new resort, styled Birchwood Arbor, so well in shape June 1, that the promised opening could be pulled off as announced. The new dancing pavilion was fully sheeted up and the windows were temporarily in place.

A chicken supper celebrated the event so far as the culinary service was concerned and it was an excellent prognostication of what the cooks can do. It was swell.

So, too, was the dance. Morgan Hough's Chateau Country Club Orchestra, engaged for the season, furnished music for their trial effort that gave the utmost pleasure and satisfaction. Finally, the financial returns of the opening night were a good starting 'heartener' for Ellsworth in his big undertaking."

-Republican-News, June 5, 1926

86

Silver Sands Resort

"The Silver Sands Resort announces its opening with a chicken dinner on Sunday. The resort plans to serve meals and quick lunches throughout the season. Special attention will be given to parties.

The resort is provided with swings, bathing privileges, spring water, etc., and those outdoor privileges are free, visitors being welcome to bring their own lunches if they wish. Ample and adequate parking space is also free."

-Republican-News, June 28, 1938

Postcard message:

Butch, we will be up here for another week of pure, unadulterated loafing! Slept 14 1/2 hours in one night! Imagine! Of course, I vary my activities a little by eating, swimming, beachcombing, eating, hiking, eating, or just plain sitting. Will wear myself out frightfully at such a rate, I know!

-Love, Lola

Postmarked Saint Ignace, 1948
Mailed to Chicago, Illinois

WAGNER'S ROADHOUSE ST. IGNACE, MICH. L-1646

Postcard message:

We are having nice weather today. Yesterday the water was too rough to go out. I caught 3 fish large enough to eat, but threw some others back. Orpha and I went swimming yesterday.

Marcia

Postmarked Saint Ignace, 1947
Mailed to Eaton, Ohio

CBLESTONE CAFE ST. IGNACE, MICH. A-530

Postcard message:

Dear Mother,

Just finished a grand dinner. Ate lunch before we got to the Straits and got the 2 o'clock boat. Our cabin is well-equipped with electric plate, dishes, percolator, etc. Right on the banks of the lake.

Love- Ella & Jim

Postmarked Saint Ignace, 1942
Mailed to Lake City, Mich.

Vitek's Restaurant

"A new modern restaurant with home cooking and baking. We serve complete breakfasts, lunches and dinners. Fried chicken and fish are our specialties. We also serve a large assortment of good sandwiches including barbeques and hamburger. Enjoy our picture window view of Mackinac Island while you eat.

927 N. STATE ST.   ST. IGNACE, MICH.
One mile north of the ferry dock on U.S. No. 2"

-Upper Peninsula Development Bureau, *The Lure Book,* 1951

VITEK'S RESTAURANT "A GOOD PLACE TO EAT - 1 MILE N. FERRY DOCK ON U.S. #2 ST. IGNACE, MICH. S-1837

Gateway to Hiawatha-land
Delightful to Visitors and All Who Live Here

The city of St. Ignace, gateway to Hiawatha-land, opens cordial welcoming arms to those who come to this delightful northland seeking recreation, health and the cool, delightful climate to be found here.

Two thousand happy people live in St. Ignace the year around. The city offers almost every inducement to the visitor to spend a vacation annually here. Golfers will revel in the excellent golf course which is overlooking the straits. Bathers will find the waters of Lake Michigan and Lake Huron, and of the immediate straits, all that they desire. And the boating facilities are unexcelled in any of the fine resorts of northern Michigan. A highly rated airport has been constructed and is attracting planes from all over the nation… St. Ignace is a paradise of the fisherman and the hunter. The health seeker and he who wants rest and quiet and beauty will find all these things in St. Ignace – together with a wonderful hospitality of those who live here."

-St. Ignace Information Bureau, *Gateway to Hiawatha-land: St. Ignace*, circa 1930

St. Ignace
In the Land of Hiawatha

"Hotels: Northern; Snyder; St. Ignace; Travelers Inn.

Restaurants: Thomas; Birchwood Arbor; Dixie; New Lunch; Evergreen Inn.

Cottages: Silver Sands; LaRocque; Mulcrone; Albright; Hulbert; Love; Grant; El Reposa; Forest Grove; Cloverland; Tourist; LaChappelle; An-We-Bin; Hilsdale; Evergreen Shores; Valier; and many others.

Garages: Gateway City; Wing's; Albright; Hemm Sales (Oakland, Pontiac); Star; Litzner. All have restrooms.

Tourist Information Bureau: Northern Hotel; Travelers Inn; Thomas Restaurant; Highstone's.

Golf: St. Ignace Golf and Country Club course, southwest of city, overlooking the Straits. Visiting Golfers Welcome. Small green fees. Complete outfits for rent. A very satisfactory course.

Airport: Just north of city, 200 acres, all-way runways. Fine gravel soil, always dry and hard.

Campsite: Straits State Park, two miles west of city on shore of Straits of Mackinac. Well-equipped, beautiful surroundings and a fine place to camp. Another summer camp is nearby at Densmore's.

Reservations and Side Trips: See information bureaus for hotel, cottage, room and garage reservations, side trips, hunting and fishing, or excursions and outings for any point in Mackinac County. No charge for this service. The St. Ignace Lions Club will be glad to arrange on application for visitor accommodations in summer homes, cottages and log cabins in or near St. Ignace."

-Vacation in St. Ignace: Hub of the Historic Straits Region, circa 1945

Nature's Grandeur Gives you Golden Sand Beaches With Air Washed Pure by the Great Lakes and Scented by Evergreen Pine and Balsam

Castle Rock on U.S. 31 near St. Ignace, Mich.
Ancient Lookout of the Ojibways

Castle Rock
Ancient Lookout of the Ojibways

"Castle Rock...is a commanding pillar of native limestone. A stairway leading to the steel lookout platform on its crest brings to you a view unsurpassed in all the Straits country. Lakes, ships, islands, hundreds of miles of forest. Powerful telescopes give close-ups of grazing deer and sometimes a fox, bear or porcupine in their native haunts. The panorama which delights the tourist's eye from this vantage point makes him realize that he has arrived in the 'Land of Sky Blue Waters'."

-Eby, C.C., *Mackinac County of the Straits Country*, circa 1925

Postcard message:

We climbed up here this morning. Could almost see to Ohio from the top. Are camping in bear and deer country tonight. Nice weather and are having a fine time. Wish you might be with us.

-Ada

Postmarked Saint Ignace, 1933
Mailed to Bolivia, Ohio

View from Castle Rock, St. Ignace, Michigan, Historic Mackinac and Round Islands in Lake Huron and the Straights of Mackinac in distance

Paul Bunyan at Castle Rock

Beneath the shadow of Castle Rock, the legendary Paul Bunyan and his blue ox, "Babe," rest after sharpening the famous axe which felled so many giant trees in the north woods. Generations of Michigan school children still love to read about this heroic lumberjack and his tall-tale adventures.

Postcard message:

We got to the Straits at 3:30 Sunday afternoon and are staying in a cabin. We went to see the Castle Rock and Indian Village. We are going to the Soo in the morning.
Clarence & Pauline

Postmarked Saint Ignace, 1948
Mailed to Casnovia, Mich.

INDIAN VILLAGE, ST. IGNACE, MICH.   4781-29

Indian Village a Star Attraction to Visitors

"One of the great tourist attractions along the historic Straits of Mackinac is the famed, genuine Indian Village at St. Ignace. It was started nearly twenty years ago, in a small way, by Clarence C. Eby and his enthusiastic wife, both students of Indian lore and craftsmanship. Today it is known all over the United States, not only for its unique original features, with wigwams, bark covered buildings and wide range of exhibits, but also as an industry where year in and year out skilled Indian men and women work on typical products which supply a national souvenir and collectors market.

The Indian Village at St. Ignace is maintained as a vital connecting link between modern civilization and the vanishing remnants of Indian arts and crafts. It is open to the public free of charge and thousands of visitors roam through its broad expanse every summer."

-*Mackinac Island News*, August 23, 1941

A CORNER IN THE INDIAN VILLAGE WAG-IN-AGON (SALES ROOM), ST. IGNACE, MICH.

HAND MADE
Indian Baskets
All Weaving Done by
Real Indians
of Local Tribes
At Indian Village

SEE THEM AT WORK!

Opposite Marquette Park

St. Ignace,   :-:   Michigan

BASKET MAKERS AT WORK AT
INDIAN VILLAGE
NEXT DOOR TO EBY'S - ST. IGNACE, MICH.

Fort Algonquin Trading Post on U.S. 31 near St. Ignace, Mich.

Fort Algonquin on U.S. 31 near St. Ignace, Mich.

Fort Algonquin

"…Fort Algonquin is a faithful reproduction of an early pioneer fort and trading post. Within the confines of its spiked stockade is a museum of interesting relics of the Indian and early white life in Northern Michigan. Ancient stone implements, flintlock guns, logging equipment and thousands of other articles of interest. Cages contain various animals native to our forests will give you an intimate view of their life. You will find Fort Algonquin historic and interesting."

-Eby, C.C.,
Mackinac County of the Straits Country,
circa 1930

DON'T FAIL TO STOP AT THIS POINT OF HISTORIC INTEREST

Accurate Reproduction of Historic French and Indian Stockade

FORT ALGONQUIN

Two Miles North of St. Ignace, Mich., on US-31
Free Museum of Indian and Other Interesting Relics
Souvenirs, Appetizing Lunches, Soft Drinks, Ice Cream, Candy, Cigars, Gas and Oil, Clean Rest Rooms.

Lovely Water-View Drive

"Westward from St. Ignace along the Straits of Mackinac and the northern shore of Lake Michigan runs one of the loveliest of Michigan's many water-view drives. It is the new concrete-paved route of US-2. This new paved way, climbing abruptly over the St. Ignace peninsula ridge, and then following the Lake Michigan beach and dunes to Brevort, offers an inspiring introduction to the Upper Peninsula… The paved highway runs directly along the beach in places, crossing the wide sand flats. So close to the water at times that one wonders what would happen if Lake Michigan's level should rise several feet. However, the pavement is well above the highest known watermark.

Wherever the prevailing westerly winds fling the waves against a Michigan shore, there are sand dunes. So the stretch along the St. Ignace peninsula from St. Ignace to Brevort with a southwestern exposure, has its hills and valleys and flats of shifting sands. Sometimes the road runs behind the dunes, sometimes between the dunes and shore, sometimes on ridges atop the dunes."

-Stace, Arthur, *Touring the Coasts of Michigan*, 1937-38

Straits State Park

"The Straits State Park, consisting of 45 acres, is located on the famous Mackinac Straits, about two miles west of the city of St. Ignace. Approximately 800 feet of the site abuts the water. The land was purchased by the public-spirited citizens of St. Ignace in co-operation with the Mackinac County Board of Supervisors. It is well developed and equipped. Park is supplied with city water and modern sanitary facilities."

-Upper Peninsula Development Bureau, *Land of Hiawatha,* circa 1934

The Mystery Spot
St. Ignace, Michigan
Location, 5 miles west of St. Ignace

"Where the law of gravity appears to have gone haywire and your idea of equilibrium is entirely upset…

It's crazy…it's perplexing…it's nature's black magic. That's why it is called the MYSTERY SPOT. The Doubting Thomas who heads for the spot finds himself puzzled when he staggers out to regain his sense of balance and perspective.

How can you explain laying a carpenter's level across 2 cement blocks noting for yourself their tops are on the same level, then standing on one and seeing your companion on the other, either above or below you.

Some say it must have been caused by an earthquake; some say there must be magnetized mineral deposits in the ground underneath. Some astonished visitors have just sworn off drinking and let it go at that.

We invite you to visit the MYSTERY SPOT, experience these natural illusions, and offer your theories. It's entertaining for young and old. A nominal admission fee is made."

-The Mystery Spot - St. Ignace, Michigan, circa 1953

Curio Fair

"Curio Fair, Northern Michigan's largest and most unique curio, novelty and souvenir store, is located two miles west of St. Ignace on scenic Highway No. 2. Printed words, however prolific, cannot possibly describe the many entirely novel and intriguing construction features. Two years in construction, the lookout tower offers a beautiful panoramic view of the Straits of Mackinac and the famous new bridge, longest suspension bridge in the world."

-Postcard back, circa 1955

Postcard message:

Susie,
Got some presents for you and Butch, something for Mom and Daddy too. They're real nice. You'll see them when we get home. Be real good and mind everyone.

Carol & Marty

Postmarked Saint Ignace, 1958
Mailed to La Salle, Ind.

Treasure Island
Pirate Treasure – Indian Museum

"Thrill to the spectacular Exhibits brought to you from the treasure trove of the azure blue waters of the Caribbean. Walk through rooms filled with Sunken Galleons of the Spanish Main. See Pieces of Eight, Golden Doubloons, Ingots of Silver and other booty of the pirates, buccaneers and freebooters who roamed the seas during the 17th Century. See the 10,000 gallon Marine Exhibit Tank – Michigan's Largest Underwater Fairyland. Walk through a wonderland of Indian curios, that capture the Savagery of the Apache, the Culture of the Pueblo and the Legends of the Chippewa. See the World's Largest Canoe. Prehistoric weapons of the Cave Man, Shrunken Heads, Apache Scalp Locks, Bundle Burials and thousands of other Relics."

-*Treasure Island, St. Ignace*, circa 1960

CHIPPEWA TOTEM VILLAGE

9 Miles West of Mackinac Bridge on US-2
Indian lore and related history in an educational and fascinating manner.

Chief White Wolf and Happy Day Woman

**Owned and Operated by
Chief White Wolf and Family**

**Indian Goods, Moccasins, Souvenirs and
Genuine Stone Relics are available at
reasonable prices**

Go West 9 Miles on US-2 from Bridge

Chippewa Totem Village
Owned and Operated by Chief White Wolf and Family

"Chief White Wolf brings the past to life through his unusual display of hand-carved totems up to 22 feet tall, panoramas of Indian life, burials, chapel in the woods, stone implements, bead work, cradle boards, snow shoes, feather work, documents, etc. Over 50 displays. It fascinates young and old. Visited by many professors, Ph. D.'s, and students of ethnology annually.

Indian goods, Moccasins, Souvenirs and Genuine Stone Relics are available at reasonable prices. It doesn't have a commercial atmosphere and we believe in all people and also what we are doing. Nine Miles West of Mackinac Bridge on US-2."

-*Chippewa Totem Village*, circa 1960

CHIPPEWA TOTEM VILLAGE
CURIOS - SOUVENIRS - INDIAN LORE

WAUB-ISH-KEE-MAH-EEN-GUN

CHIEF WHITE WOLF
RALPH E. McCARRY

PUBLIC LECTURER

PHONE 89-W1
ST. IGNACE, MICH.

Chapter Five — Mackinac Island

Mackinac Island, "the Gem of the Great Lakes," rises out of the Straits of Mackinac between Lake Michigan and Lake Huron. About eight miles in circumference, it covers 2,221 acres. Its main plateau is 150 feet above the level of the surrounding waters and the highest point reaches 339 feet.

The Island was called Michilimackinac, meaning "great turtle" by the Native Americans. One legend relates that a large gathering of Native Americans was assembled at St. Ignace, and while gazing at the rising sun, during the great Manitou, or February moon, they beheld the Island suddenly rise up out of the water, assuming its present form. From their point of view, it resembled the back of a large turtle. Over time the name was shortened to Mackinac.

Because of its strategic location on the Straits, the Island was a gathering place for Native Americans, an assembly place for intertribal meetings and a refuge for tribes fleeing from the Iroquois. The Native Americans tribes in the region were the Ottawa (Odawa) and the Chippewa (Ojibway). They camped on its shores during the warmer months, hunting and fishing in the fertile local waters, and trading some of their harvest for grains and vegetables offered by Native American tribes to the south. After the Treaty of 1836, Mackinac Island was designated as the place for the annual annuity payments to be made to thousands of Native Americans by the U.S. government. The Island was a busy place in the early 1800s, populated with Native Americans and fur traders. John Jacob Astor established his American Fur Trading Company in 1809 and began amassing his great fortune. As the fur trade diminished, Astor sold the business. When the company closed its operation in 1842, the Island population dropped sharply. Meanwhile the fishing industry became increasingly vital. From the late 1840s to the early 1880s the Island was a center of the fishing industry of the Great Lakes, packing and shipping whitefish and Mackinaw trout all over the Midwest. As commercial fishing declined some fishermen began to charter sport fishing expeditions for the tourists who started to visit the Island after the Civil War. Soon the economy of the Island was based on tourism.

Although only a few white visitors had come to the Island in the first half of the 19th century, their writings later helped to popularize the Island as a tourist destination. Among these early travelers were several writers, including Alexis De Tocqueville, Harriet Martineau, Margaret Fuller and William Cullen Bryant. They praised the Island's beauty, healthful climate, and interesting features. Captain Marryatt, a renowned officer in the British navy and popular novelist of the time, recorded in his 1837 *Diary in America* this about Mackinac Island: "It has the appearance of a fairy island floating on the water, which is so pure and transparent that you may see down to any depth, and the air above is as pure as the water, that you feel invigorated as you breathe it." Miss Martineau, a woman of high rank and literary distinction, wrote of Mackinac Island, "It is known to me as the wildest and tenderest piece of beauty that I have yet seen on God's earth." Such praise of the Island bolstered the tourist industry after the Civil War. The first travel guide to the island appeared in 1875, followed by a flood of publicity in newspapers, magazines, and steamship and railroad travel brochures.

In the late 19th century, Midwesterners began summering on Mackinac, responding to the call of its charms. They came by steamships from Detroit, Cleveland, Chicago, Duluth and Montreal. Steamship lines started to make Mackinac Island one of their main ports in the 1870s and 1880s. In 1890 the Detroit & Cleveland Steam Navigation Company offered a scenic three-day cruise from Detroit to the Island for $4.00 per day. The fast steamships delivered fresh food to the Island three times a week. However, the steamships did not have a monopoly on passenger traffic.

Railroad service reached Mackinaw City and St. Ignace in 1881 and made connections throughout the country, bringing visitors from such cities as Cincinnati, Boston, and New Orleans. Ferry service from both sides of the Straits was inaugurated in 1881 by the Arnold Transit Company. This made an easy trip for those railroad passengers traveling to the Island. In response to the Island's growing reputation as a beauty spot and summer resort, in 1875 the U.S. government created Mackinac National Park. It was the second park created after Yellowstone. The park was put under the control of the Commandant of Fort Mackinac. The Island's new status as a National Park attracted even more crowds of summer tourists.

Early visitors to the Island found a few hotels, including the Mission House (1850), the Island House (1852), and the Lake View House (1858). As the tourist trade grew, these few hotels could not accommodate all the visitors. The former American Fur Trading Company was converted into the John Jacob Astor Hotel in the 1870s. More hotels were built over the next several decades: the Murray Hotel (1882), the Chippewa Hotel (1902), the Iroquois Hotel (1902) and several others. Boardinghouses also added to the Island's inventory of accommodations.

The colossal Grand Hotel opened in 1887. In the interest of bringing more visitors to the Island, three transportation companies joined forces to finance the hotel. Under the management of John Oliver Plank, an outstanding resort hotel operator at the time, the Detroit & Cleveland Navigation Company, the Grand Rapids & Indiana Railway and the Michigan Central Railroad formed the Mackinac Island Hotel Company and designated Cornelius Vanderbilt as president. The hotel was advertised as "Plank's Grand Hotel" until 1890 when Plank sold his interest. The Grand Hotel set a standard of excellence for summer hotels across the country. It offered fine dining, orchestra music and an elegant ballroom for dancing, strolls along the "world's longest porch" and walks through its beautifully landscaped grounds. More amenities were added over the years. For the sports-minded there was swimming, golf, tennis, horseback riding and, of course, bicycling.

Visitors used a variety of ways to get around the Island. The bicycle craze of the Gay 90s found a hearty response with Islanders and visitors alike. By 1896 a six-foot bicycle path was completed around the Island. Horseback riding also became a popular pastime. The first automobile arrived on the Island in 1898 and threatened to change the quiet life on the village streets. The carriage drivers protested these horseless carriages and petitioned the Village Council to ban automobiles and a formal ordinance was passed. Three years later, in 1901, the Mackinac Island State Park Commission prohibited automobiles within the park limits. The ban on automobiles has successfully preserved the Victorian atmosphere of the Island.

The Island's popularity as a "fashionable watering place" drew the interest of affluent Midwesterners desiring summer cottages. Three cottage communities developed. Hubbard's Annex was built on private property, while the East and West Bluff cottages were built on land leased from the Mackinac National Park. In the 1890s wealthy capitalists from Chicago, Detroit, Grand Rapids and Kalamazoo built palatial Victorian summer homes; some of these "cottages" had 30 rooms, with additional carriage houses and stables.

In 1895 the U.S. government turned the Island over to the State of Michigan to be used as a state park under the control of the Mackinac Island State Park Commission. The Commission was given the task of preserving Mackinac Island State Park's special character, natural wonders and historic landmarks. The first task at hand was preserving Fort Mackinac and work was begun on this long-term project. The Commission converted the old soldiers' garden in front of the fort to Marquette Park and a bronze statue of Pere Marquette was dedicated with great fanfare in 1909.

Mackinac Island flourished from the 1880s through the 1920s. The Mackinac Island Chamber of Commerce was formed in the mid-1920s to promote Mackinac as a vacation destination and succeeded in attracting even more visitors. Even Prohibition didn't stop vacationers from enjoying their time on the Island. Then the stock market Crash and the Depression brought hard times. Few tourists came, hotels suffered, ferries cut back on their service, stores closed and cottage owners defaulted on their leases. The records of the Grand Hotel show that on a July day in 1939 the hotel had only 11 registered guests, with a staff of 400. The drought continued as recreational travel throughout the country slowed down during World War II when gas and tire rationing went into effect.

The economy recovered after the war and more people had the money and the time to take vacations. Travel by automobile was favored over travel by trains or steamships. Improvements were made in Michigan's highways and additional car ferries were added at the Straits. The Mackinac Island ferryboats increased their runs. The Island saw a resurgence of tourists and business prospered. Hotels were often booked to capacity. Empty storefronts were filled with new shops and restaurants that catered to tourists. Souvenirs, curios, and candy were popular purchases. The Chamber of Commerce was revitalized. The State of Michigan purchased an Island summer home for the Governor in 1945. Jimmy Durante and Esther Williams filmed the 1947 movie, *This Time for Keeps* at the Grand Hotel.

The revitalized tourist trade threatened the very attractions the visitors came to see. People realized that the historic charm of the Island needed to be preserved. With meager state funds, the Mackinac Island State Park Commission turned to private partners in the restoration of two buildings. In the 1950s the Michigan Medical Society financed the restoration of the Beaumont Memorial, and the Michigan Society of Architects restored the Biddle House, one of the oldest private residences on the Island. Meanwhile the Mackinac Island State Park Commission worked on the restoration of the Mission Church and several other buildings. The largest project would be the continued restoration of Fort Mackinac. Following the example of the Mackinac Bridge Authority, the Commission issued revenue bonds to finance the expensive project. In 1958 the restored fort was opened to the public. The admission fee of 50 cents for adults and 25 cents for children raised $54,119 in the first year, enough to repay the entire debt. Over the years additional restoration has been done, museum exhibits created and historic demonstrations performed. From the early days of the Native Americans, the explorers and fur traders, to the days of military occupation and the growth of tourism, Mackinac Island has retained its natural beauty and historic charm. A sixteen-minute ferry ride to the Island takes one back hundreds of years in time to this land of living history.

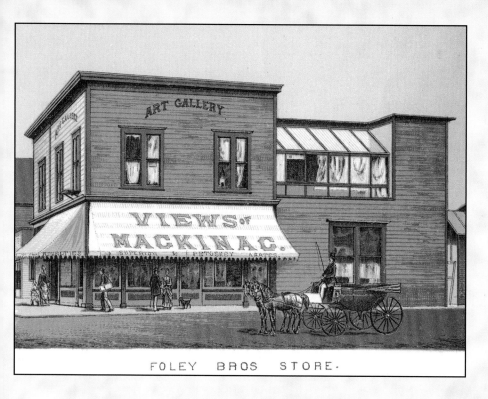

FOLEY BROS STORE.

Photographic Souvenirs

The blossoming of Mackinac Island into a tourist destination paralleled the development of photography in America. The earliest photographic souvenirs were stereo cards and cabinet cards made by regional commercial studios, usually from Detroit or Chicago, which wholesaled their wares to Island shops. In the 1880s Henry J. Rossiter and the Foley Brothers started photography businesses on Mackinac Island. They sold their photographic views directly to Island gift and souvenir stores. Unfortunately, the Foley Brothers studio burned in 1895, along with its stock. The business was relocated to Petoskey. Over the following decades the busy tourist business drew other photographers who made photographic souvenirs of the Island.

In the late 1890s two of the Island's most prominent photographers opened up studios. William H. Gardiner and George Wickham produced stereo cards, cabinet cards and portraits primarily to sell to tourists as mementos of their trip. They also produced pictorial souvenir booklets of Island scenes. When stereo cards went out of favor in the early 1900s, both studios started making postcards. Postcards were immensely popular with Island tourists. It's likely that thousands of postcards were mailed each week from Mackinac Island at the height of the postcard craze (1908-1920). Quite possibly just as many went home as souvenirs, to be kept in albums on parlor tables to show the folks back home.

Photographic studios often had props or elaborate backgrounds to use in creating comic or whimsical portraits. Paper moons, boats, autos or hot-air balloons tempted tourists to have unique portraits made. These four chaps, photographed by an unknown studio, were "Flying High at Mackinac Island."

Early Travel Guides

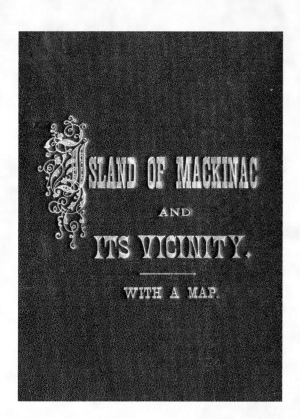

Although Mackinac Island had seen a steady stream of travelers since the Civil War, it wasn't until 1875 that the first travel guide to the Island was published. J. Disturnell's *Island of Mackinac and Its Vicinity* set the standard for the many guidebooks that followed. He gave information on transportation to the Island, lodging, climate and natural features. Disturnell's history of the Island was written with the curious visitor in mind. He included "Places worth seeing on the Island." He also noted of the "necessity that a magnificent hotel should be, at an early date, erected in this favorite watering place." The success of Disturnell's book spurred many other guides, including *Souvenir of Mackinac Island* which was printed on birch bark about 1890. The *Standard Guide to Mackinac Island and Northern Lake Resorts* was a popular guide in the early 1900s. Railroad and steamship lines of this period also featured Mackinac Island as a vacation destination in their promotional publications.

"In the compilation of this WORK the Author has been influenced by the desire of numerous individuals to have prepared an ILLUSTRATED GUIDE to this favorite resort, now attracting more than ever the attention of the invalid and the seekers of pleasure, as well as the capitalists, who are interested in steamboat lines, and those engaged in the construction of railroads…thereby affording pleasant and speedy access to this hitherto neglected region of country, where health prevails."

Disturnell, J., *The Island of Mackinac and Its Vicinity,* 1875

Native Americans from the Mackinac region sit along the docks on Mackinac Island selling their crafts to tourists for souvenirs, circa 1890.

MACKINAC
INDIAN BAZAAR.

STRANGERS & VISITORS

To this charming and Romantic Island, for ages the Paradise of the Genii, so believed from time immemorial by the Indian Tribes, wishing to procure a Souvenir of their visit to the "FAIRY ISLE," the spiritual resting-place of the departed Braves and renowned Warriors of the West, will find a rare and splendid collection of

GENUINE INDIAN CURIOSITIES,
Of all descriptions at the Indian Bazaar.

FENTON & WENDELL, Proprietors,
MACKINAC, MICH.

June, 1875.
96)

Native Americans

Native Americans were, of course, the first summer "vacationers" on Mackinac Island, long before the first Europeans came to the region. Centuries ago, Native Americans made long summer voyages to the Island to enjoy its charms. By some accounts, it was considered a sacred place where many ceremonies and rituals were conducted.

By the mid 1880s, public interest and curiosity about Native Americans were growing. Island stores capitalized on this interest and the tourists' desire for souvenirs made by local Native Americans. In 1875, Highstone's Indian Curiosity Store advertised "Bark Boxes, Trunks, and Baskets of every description. Sweet Grass in every variety of work, Bead Work, Feathers, Fans, Ladies' Bark Hats, etc. The assortment including every description of Fancy Work made by Chippewa Indians." Fenton & Wendell's Mackinac Indian Bazaar also featured "Genuine Indian Curiosities" as souvenirs of the "Fairy Isle, the spiritual resting-place of the departed Braves and renowned Warriors of the West."

VIEW OF THE TOWN OF MACKINAW.

Tide of Travel of Summer Visitors

"A short score of years ago but a few hundred travelers in each summer had visited one spot in Northern Michigan – Mackinac Island. Such had found that beautiful isle so delightful a resort they were regular summer visitors. Since those days, so great has become the tide of travel of summer visitors in Northern Michigan, during 1890 nearly quite or quite one hundred thousand found renewed health and strength among the beautiful lakes, and the health-giving breezes of the most delightful resort region in all America. Such know the way and will return year after year, for them no other land presents so many and such varied attractions."

-*Mackinac the Wonderful Isle*, 1891

Important Health Resort

"The island is the most important summer resort to which we can direct the attention of the infirm or the fashionable. As a health resort it is unsurpassed. Its cool, dry air and the living streams of pure water which gush from the lime rock precipices, are just what are needed to bring back the glow of health to the faded check, and send the warm currents of life dancing through the system, superceding all necessity for nauseating iron, sulphur and Epsom salts… You eat with a new relish, and sleep like a child. You row, or ramble, scarcely able to keep your buoyancy within bounds. Dr. Mills, once post surgeon of Mackinac, says: 'No better place can be found for sickly girls and puny boys, for worn-out men and women'."

-Detroit & Cleveland Navigation Co., *Midsummer Voyages on Northern Seas,* circa 1890

The Wonderful Isle

"Mackinac Island…has the most equable, exhilarating and delightful summer climate of any spot in the north temperate zone… The Wonderful Island, surrounded by the blue-green waters which separate the two peninsulas composing the State of Michigan, has all the beauties and advantages of an ideal summer resort. This has been known for centuries, for the aboriginal inhabitants of the Peninsular State regarded the island as the especial home of the 'Great Spirit'. It was as near an approximation of heaven as the Indian had ever realized. So imagery and metaphor have been exhausted in the vain attempt to describe its glories. It has been named 'The Wonderful Isle,' 'The Queen of Enchantment,' 'The Tourists' Paradise,' 'Gem of the Straits,' 'The Fairy Island' - indeed it has almost as many pet names as it has had visitors, and their number is legion."

-Mackinac, the Wonderful Isle, circa 1892

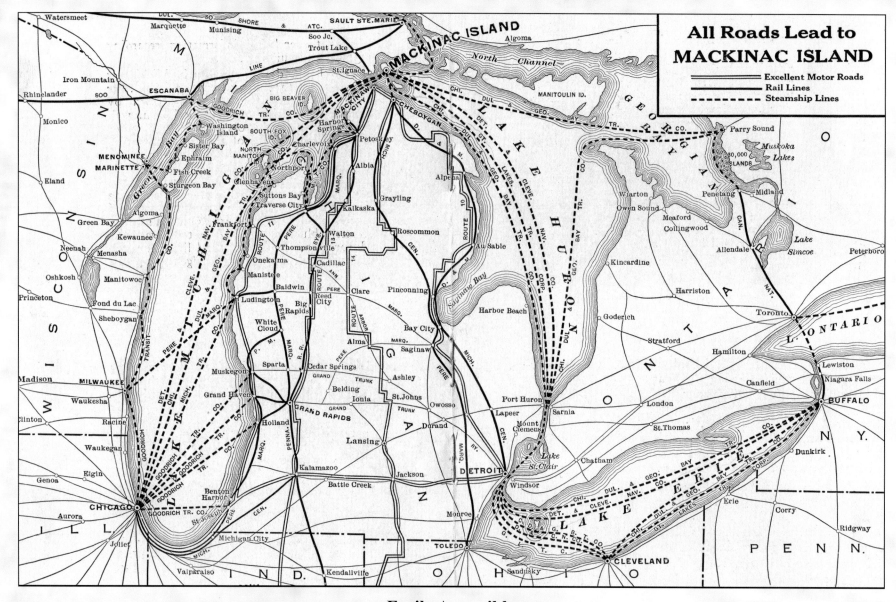

Easily Accessible

"Mackinac Island stands high and proud in the Straits of Mackinac, between Lake Michigan and Lake Huron and within reach of the crisp, cool breezes that blow south from Lake Superior…

Mackinac Island has unusual transportation facilities. Ten steamer lines operate twenty-five first-class steamers regularly between the Island and all principal lake ports. Steamers are run with such frequency as to suit the pleasure of practically every traveler from Buffalo, Cleveland, Toledo, Detroit, Duluth, Chicago and Milwaukee. Four large railroad systems run solid Pullman trains several times daily from all points south, east, west and north."

-Mackinac Island Michigan, circa 1920

Hub of Activity

The docks were the center of all the Island's activities. Communications, travelers and the life-blood of commerce arrived at the docks. Steamships brought tourists and visitors to the Island, as well as all the necessities of life: food, clothing, medicine, building materials and, of course, merchandise for the gift and souvenir shops. It was a favorite activity for Islanders and tourists alike to watch the parade of ships and passengers arriving at the Island's docks.

Arnold's Dock, Mackinac Island, Mich.

Postcard message:

Dear Mary,
This is where our boat lands
on the island. Could spend a
fortune in this town.
— *Dorothy*

Postmarked
Mackinac Island, 1921
Mailed to Lansing. Mich.

Splendid Steamers

"In addition to the benefits to be derived by a stay upon the island, the hygienic influences of the journey there on splendid steamers plying from our main ports on the lakes is to be considered. While en route inhaling the inspiring air of the lakes, and enjoying the motion of the vessel, and with the ever varying conditions of the trip, you feel a new tidal wave of life sweep over your frame, and when you leave the island, after a stay there of a few weeks, you feel like 'a strong man ready to run a race'."

-Robinson, George, *History of Cheboygan and Mackinac Counties*, 1873

Departure of D. & C. Steamer. Mackinac Island, Mich.

Restful, Soothing Playgrounds

"Among the resorts, summer and winter, of the United States there are few such restful, soothing playgrounds for the tired city dweller as Mackinac Island. Here there is no smoke of industry, no hustle and bustle of commerce, no noise of speeding railroad trains or trolley cars, no chugging taxis… Yet the quiet of Mackinac is not freighted with lonesomeness. The soothing winds from off the lakes, bustling through the pines and hemlocks, inspire rest and relaxation, and at the comfortable hotels and cottages, refined congeniality prevails. Here the cultured family from St. Louis meets the equally cultured and companionable family from Cincinnati or Chicago."

-U.S. Railroad Administration, *Michigan Summer Resorts,* circa 1920

Cool Beauty Spot of the World

"No Hay Fever, no malaria, no mosquitoes or other insect pests…will be found on the 'Fairy' Isle. It is impossible to put into language a word picture which will bring to mind the many beauties and attractions which combine to make Mackinac Island 'the cool beauty spot of the world.'

Convenient of access, delightfully situated, endowed by Nature with great beauty, rich in legendary lore and historical facts, Mackinac Island claims first place among the resorts of America."

-East Michigan Tourist Association, *East Michigan Tourist Guide*, 1932

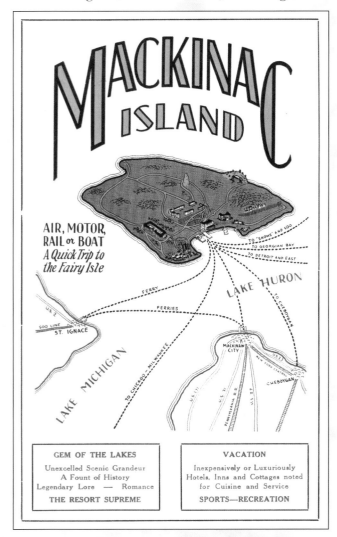

OLD INDIAN TRAIL, MACKINAC ISLAND, MICH.   A-7102

Postcard message:

Sunday
This is no place for a Ford, Dodge, Reo or Buick. They and no other
machines are allowed in this picturesque place. This island seems a thousand
miles from nowhere - a great place and would like to have more time here.
                                                    - Love, Gladys

Postmarked Mackinac Island, 1927
Mailed to Indianapolis, Ind.

VIEW OF MACKINAC ISLAND AND HARBOR.

Famous Scenery

"The Island is justly famed for its scenery. The heights command views of sea and shore, ever changing with the varying lights and shades of the hours and the movements of passing ships. Well kept roads – thirty miles of them – lead in various directions from the village, through the woods, amid curious rock formations, now along the edge of the bluff with vistas of the lake, and again to some open outlook, whence the panorama is bounded only by the limitations of vision. There are glens and ravines innumerable; open spaces which were the ancient gardens of the Indians; and delectable parks, whose clumps of shrubs and trees are so effectively arranged that one at first credits the artistic effect to the skill of landscape artist rather than to the caprice of nature."

-Standard Guide, Mackinac Island and Northern Lake Resorts, 1904

Postcard message:

Dear Anna,
Ed and I are doing the hay fever act once more. Are in the middle
of Lake Huron and the cold is intense. Ed was real bad when we
started from home at 3 yesterday – but is easier now. We could see
plenty of white sea gulls following the boat, and begging for scraps.
Are two hundred and forty state rooms on this steamer and all
are full. It is the "City of Mackinac." Expect soon to see the place
pictured on the other side.

Love to your dear mother and all- Ella

Postmarked Mackinac Island, 1911
Mailed to Menlo, Iowa

Modern Conveniences

"The main street of the town of Mackinac is lined with shops of every description. The presence of all-summer cottagers, campers and transient hotel guests is recognized in the complete stocks of groceries, provisions, dry goods and furnishings. Curio and auction stores are especially attractive.

During the months of June, July, August and September there are seven daily mails, both in and out. Telegraph and long-distance telephone connect the Island with all parts of the country and make it possible for a man to take a perfect vacation and keep in touch with his business at the same time. An excellent system of water works is in operation throughout the year, a modern sewer system is connected with every house, and streets and houses are lighted by electricity."

-Mackinac Island, Michigan, circa 1920

Mackinac Island Shopping

"A stroll along the Island's business street shows more activity and new developments than ever… Both the Carriage Lantern Tea room and the Doud Mercantile Company have expanded into adjoining space. The Carriage Lantern, besides specializing in unusually good chicken pies, has now developed appetizing box lunches for the convenience of bicyclists, hikers and picnickers in general. Doud's has put in a complete line of frozen fruits and vegetables… And down the street toward the post office, is a new shop, the National Photo Service; here you may have your picture snapped as you start out in an Island carriage, and find it ready to pick up when you return from your drive. As usual, Mr. George H. Wickman has a distinctive shop, with glassware, curios and costume jewelry to interest the discriminating shopper. The John S. Doud Curio Store specializes, as always, in fine Indian goods and balsam pillows… Opposite the post office Clarice McKeever's Studio is starting another season with a delightful, large-size map of the Island that should be a 'must' on everyone's shopping list."

-The Island News, July 5, 1947

Mackinac Eating Places

For Real Grecian or Italian
SPAGHETTI
Stop at the
Astor Cafe
Try Our Famous Greek Salad
Phone 4671 for Reservations

"Many of the Mackinac Island eating places are noted for their home cooking. Mrs. Emmerts serves three delicious home cooked meals a day. Mrs. Leslie O'Brien, of O'Brien's Rendezvous, serves especially good turkey dinners. If you want just a snack, what could be better than the Snack Bar, near the Grand Hotel. They serve sandwiches all during the day and late into the evening. Some other good places for sandwiches are Bartlings on the dock, which has wonderful cheese sandwiches, and Truscotts, which serves Canadian bacon sandwiches that are a joy to eat.

The Astor Café specializes in real Grecian or Italian spaghetti. Mary's Pantry, which is half way up to the Grand, serves good old southern fried chicken, as well as deliciously prepared fish. Miss Orma Squires, head waitress at the Lakeview Hotel dining room for 14 years, tells us that they are serving especially good prime ribs of beef. They also have excellent steaks and turkey."

-The Island News, July 22, 1948

The Land of Fudge

Mackinac Island is known as the "land of fudge," the Island's only exported product. The sweet smell of fudge has perfumed the air of the Island since 1889 when the Murdick family opened Murdick's Candy Kitchen, the first store on the Island to sell only candy. The family saw the growth of tourism on the Island and seized the opportunity to cater to the sweet tooth of the Victorian summer visitor. Other fudge stores followed over the years, including May's in 1930 and Ryba's in 1960. While other fudge shops displayed their fudge-making process in the back of their stores, Ryba's moved the demonstration to the front window of its store. Tourists were fascinated, watching the sweet ingredients mixed in large copper kettles, heated, and then poured onto large marble slabs to cool. The confectioners then worked quickly, creaming the fudge, mixing it with long-handled spatulas and working the mixture into blocks. In the 1960s Ryba's coined the term "fudgie" for Island visitors and the term has stuck ever since. With a small number of year-round residents, "fudgies" are the sweetest ingredient in Mackinac Island's economy.

Postcard message:

Dear Marian,
Finally made it here. Over 300 miles of bumpy riding. Took boat over to Island. Staying at a nice hotel. Went shopping this morning, you would like the quaint stores - lots of souvenirs and fudge. Will go swimming this afternoon and dancing tonight. having a wonderful time, it is so beautiful here. No cars, only horses and bikes. No flies or mosquitoes. It is a little cool tho.

Love, Joanie

Postmarked Mackinac Island, 1954
Mailed to Holland, Mich.

The Official Carriage Tour of Mackinac Island

OFFICIAL CARRIAGE TOUR
HISTORIC SCENIC POINTS OF INTEREST
FEATURING OLD FORT MACKINAC

CARRIAGE TOUR TICKETS

Historic Scenic Points of Interest Featuring Old Fort Mackinac

A carefully planned 1½ hour carriage ride to more than 30 points of scenic and historic interest.

Ticket Office and Carriages are at the center of Main Street, next to Chamber of Commerce Information Office.

FARES: Adults, $2.50—Children under 12, $1.00—Under 5, FREE.

Visit famous Fort Mackinac. See the most historic spot in Michigan. The museums and exhibits make history live again. Last stop on carriage tour.

Pleasant drivers to describe points of interest and to answer your questions.

Postcard message:

Dear Jane Dorothy,
Have had a wonderful day here, had lunch at the Grand Hotel, then took the 7-mile tour of the Island in a surrey. They keep 50 surreys in use all the time. No cars allowed. It's the summer home spot of the rich. Sun shining but on the cool side. You would like it here.

Rita

Postmarked Mackinac Island, 1954
Mailed to Denver, Colorado

Carriage Men To Show Island Visitors All Historic Sights

"The clip-clop of horses' hoofs is one of the first sounds that greets the ears of visitors to Mackinac Island. Many of them, new to the Island, had forgotten, almost, what a carriage looks like while others of the younger generation take their first 'buggy' ride while visiting here. The Mackinac Island Carriage Men's Association provides a large number of horses and carriages for trips around the Island, through its shady lanes and past its points of historical and scenic interest. Drivers, carefully picked, are courteous and accommodating and give lectures on points of historical interest.

The carriage drives wind along the rocky shore, through wooded glades and along high crests. Included in the drives are points of major interest such as Arch Rock, British Landing, Sugar Loaf, old forts of intensely interesting background, the historical museum and many other points of interest.

There are no automobiles on the Island, but the Carriage Men's Association has supplied a novel, comfortable and quiet means of transportation that goes with the quaint charm of the Island."

-Mackinac Islander, June 2, 1935

119

Speed Boats Thrill Thousands Annually

"Thousands of summer tourists each year at Mackinac Island have experienced their first thrill of gliding over the crystal blue waters of the Great Lakes. There are ten commercial speed crafts operating in and out of the local harbor continuously during the day. Three of these boats circumnavigate the Island. The others operate on schedule between the Island and mainland. Two run between Mackinac Island and Mackinaw City, while there are five which ply the waters between the Island and St. Ignace. Several of these boats are available for special trips and it is not unusual for a group of vacationers to charter one of these speed crafts for an afternoon or evening cruise. All are under the command of capable licensed pilots."

-Mackinac Island News, July 16, 1938

Cycling is Popular

"Bicycle riding on Mackinac Island offers a safe, healthy and enjoyable means of travel to both visitors and residents, and for fun and recreation, there is no better pastime.

Summer guests of hotels and cottages on the Island are much in evidence pedaling about the cool shore roads, while the hardier riders venture forth to the hills' trails.

There are no traffic hazards on the Fairy Isle, which makes this sport all the more enjoyable."

-*Mackinac Island News*, July 8, 1939

NO AUTOS ON MACKINAC ISLAND . . .
RIDE A BIKE from
ISLAND BICYCLE LIVERY
New Wheels rented by day or hour.
——:——
"Around Mackinac Island" Speed Boats

Postcard message:

Boy, we really gave ourselves a workout today. Riding a bicycle "built for two" all the way around the Mackinac Island really wears you out. I wore a hole right through my white flats today from doing so much walking and bicycle riding. Tonight we are going swimming.

Love, Jerry & Mary

Postmarked Mackinac Island, date not legible
Mailed to East Detroit, Mich.

Greetings from Mackinac Island.

Annual Mackinac Races

"The annual Mackinac races, from Detroit and Chicago, are the outstanding fresh water events of the yachting world. They serve to focus the eyes of the nation on Mackinac Island, where between 40 and 60 yachts each year cross the finishing line to the accompaniment of booming cannon and cheering spectators.

Spectators come by rail, airplane, steamer and yacht to be at the finish. The harbor, one of the finest on the Great Lakes, is crowded with craft, some little more than oversize rowboats, others gilded, steam or diesel playthings of the rich. When the racing yachts are in, the harbor is packed with craft, and viewed from the heights of Fort Mackinac, it takes on the appearance of a forest of masts.

The trophies offered in the race are the most highly prized of any offered in fresh water racing events...

But Mackinac Island is the mecca of yachtsmen at other times than during the July yacht races. From the middle of June to the middle of September, cruising vessels come into the harbor, improved by the federal government during the past few years to make easy accommodations of the largest lake vessels... Many of the famous private yachts owned in Detroit, Chicago and Cleveland make frequent summer stops at Mackinac Island, riding at anchor in the famous harbor."

-Mackinac Island News, Summer, 1936

Lilac Day Festival

"Mackinac Island, June 20, 1948 – Celebration of Lilac Day as an annual observance on the Island is an event of first importance on the Mackinac calendar. The French lilacs were planted here in the earliest days and many of these famous lilac trees still survive and produce a shower of bloom; more recent lilac plantings of choice, double and single varieties, fill every yard and garden from Decoration Day until late in June with flowers and fragrance. Mackinac's climate and soil not only produce the finest lilac blooms in the country, the fresh cool air keeps lilacs in full, perfect flower for an usually long season.

Sprays of lilacs will be sold today all along the Main Street from the Chippewa to the Lakeview… Every business firm along the street has planned original lilac displays for its show windows. Every horse and carriage on the street will be decorated with lilacs.

A Lilac Day parade will start at the School House at 2 P.M. and follow the Main Street up to the Grand Hotel…"

-The Island News, July 22, 1948

MAIN STREET, MACKINAC ISLAND AT LILAC TIME, MACKINAC ISLAND, MICH.

June Brings Lilacs to Mackinac Island

"During June the Island is literally a mass of white and purple lilac blooms which lade the air with their perfume. Lilac bushes, many of them years old which have grown to trees rather than bushes, are common to the Island, but it is only in June that their color brings the realization of the number of lilacs growing on the Fairy Isle."

-Mackinac Island News, June 21, 1936

SUGAR LOAF ROCK
AND ISLAND DRIVE,
MACKINAC ISLAND, MICH.

Wonders of the Island

"Arch Rock is one of the wildest, weirdest sublimest freaks of Nature's handiwork in sculpture. The chisel-prints of untold ages of whirling water are all over it. The first glimpse of its manifold grandeurs and beauties takes away the breath of any party of intelligent tourists, and each feels, in his astonishment and delight, the inability to express the emotions that overwhelm one in the presence of such a scene. Imagine, if you can, projecting from the face of a cliff two hundred feet high, a gigantic bay window of stone, supported by a mighty arch a hundred and forty-nine feet high at its summit. The rim or wall of the bay window is about three feet wide, and it bulges out some twenty feet from the cliff, overhanging the blue-green water of the lake a dizzy depth below… Foolish people walk around the top of this narrow ledge… The view from the summit of the arch takes in a glorious sweep of fifty miles…

About a mile from Arch Rock, directly toward the centre of the Island, and standing alone amid the forest trees, is Sugar Loaf Rock, a gray, moss-grown rock towering two hundred and eighty-four feet above the lake. At the base it is, perhaps, seventy-five feet long by fifty wide. Twenty or thirty feet from the ground, on the north side of the rock, is a cave that is reached by a ladder, and venturesome people sometimes climb to the apex of the huge pyramid, more for the pleasure of saying that they have done so than for the magnificent view from the summit."

-Michigan Central Railroad, *The Fairy Isle of Mackinac,* circa 1888

LOVERS LEAP, MACKINAC ISLAND, MICH.

Natural Curiosities

"Devil's Kitchen: Limestone cave. One of the delights of the Island. A favorite place for tourists to roast marshmallows. The water rises and falls so that the entrance below is sometimes closed by high water.

Lover's Leap: Limestone pillar detached from cliff. This lone pinnacle rises to a height of 145 feet above the waters of Lake Huron, about a mile west of the main part of the city. It derives its name from a beautiful Indian legend of the Ojibways."

-Michigan Historical Commission, *Names of Places of Interest on Mackinac Island,* 1916

7533. Devil's Kitchen, Lake Shore Drive, Mackinac Island, Mich.

Postcard message:

Mackinac Island Aug. 28, 1912
Dear Franklyn-
Mr. McCarty and I are here for the hay fever. This cave in the rocks is down on the shore. The tourists build fires of driftwood in there on the rocks. A large steamer got fast on the reef of Ten Shoals and had to send to Sault Ste. Marie to get a lighter and tugs, then they worked all day pulling her off. She had 220 passengers.

Truly yours, E. McCarty

Postmarked Mackinac Island, 1912
Mailed to Lincoln, Nebraska

12074 LOOKING DOWN FROM THE OLD FORT, MACKINAC ISLAND, MICH.

COPR. DETROIT PUBLISHING CO.

Postcard message:

Dear Folks,
We are safe and sound. Arrived on the island this morning.
Everything is just as beautiful as the picture on this postcard.
Certainly something to see, so many points of interest.
-Gertie & Sam

Postmarked Mackinac Island, 1916
Mailed to Philadelphia, Pennsylvania

Old Fort Mackinac

"The village and fort of Mackinac are situated on the southeastern extremity of the island, where there is a good harbor protected by a water battery. The island remained in possession of the British from 1790 (when the fort was moved from Mackinaw City and located here) until 1793, when it was surrendered to the United States. It was retaken in 1812, but restored again by the Treaty of Ghent, in 1814… The fort which had been occupied by a regiment of troops, was, in 1896, deserted as a military station, and was granted to the State of Michigan for the purpose of a State Park."

-Hudson, Roberts,
Michigan: a Summer and Health Resort State, 1898

FORT MACKINAC, BUILT IN 1780, IS SITUATED 133 FEET ABOVE THE WATER AND COMMANDS THE TOWN HARBOR AND STRAITS.

9883   THE FORT AND STATE PARK, MACKINAC ISLAND, MICH.   COPR. DETROIT PUBLISHING CO.

Postcard message:

Visited this old fort June 20, 1908. Of special interest because of its age and historic value. There were old, old houses with their old-fashioned fireplaces, windows, doors, wrought iron nails (made by hand), etc. etc. Saw an old-fashioned knocker on one door. One large house was open and we went in and wandered about in the quaint old rooms.

Postcard not mailed.

Fort is Dominating Feature of the Island

"Fort Mackinac, on the heights above the village, is one of the dominating features of the island landscape. It is situated on an elevation 133 feet above the water, and commands the town and harbor and Straits. The parapets and old-time blockhouses have an air delightfully antiquated and picturesque. Thousands of visitors ascend the steep slope every year to make exploration of its quaint construction and arrangement. The cedar stockade with its loopholes for musketry fell to decay long ago; parapet and blockhouse have been dismantled of their guns, and no sentry challenges approach… The officers' quarters, the barracks, commissary's stores and other buildings, no longer used for military purposes have lost their martial air; some of the dwellings are occupied as summer homes. But the masonry of the fort is little changed. The stone-works have been cemented and solidified with the lapse of time; the fort seems to have become part of the hill on which it stands. In all material respects as an island stronghold, the fortification endures today as it was in those earlier years when it had part in the troubled conflicts of international strife."

-Standard Guide to Mackinac Island and Northern Lake Resorts, 1902

SOUTH SALLY PORT

America's Gibraltar

"Fort Mackinac, America's Gibraltar, once the embattled gateway to the Northwest and its rich fur trade, today stands, a quiet shrine, where students of history and lovers of peace and nature, pilgrimage… Fort Mackinac exemplifies a strange blending of the past and the present…and today stands the center of interest of Mackinac Island, Michigan's most historic spot, which has been under three flags. Here come thousands of visitors annually, to renew their love of the past, or to view the glorious vista of the harbor below… Neat, clean, whitewashed buildings are the rule. Everything is kept as near like it was in the days of military occupancy as possible.

No matter what changes the years may bring in the lives and habits of men, the magnificent view from Fort Mackinac will remain ever enthralling…"

-*Mackinac Island News,* Summer, 1936

Postcard message:

Willis-
We were at this fort today — exploring the old buildings, cannons, etc. A wonderful view from up there. Where we go from here I don't know. We caught some fish and ate all of them. We may be home next week. Keep the home fire burning 'til we get home.

Love, Mom & Dad

Postmarked Mackinac Island, 1966
Mailed to Elmwood, Indiana

Fort Mackinac Preserved

"Behind the palisaded walls and stone-flanked gates the past comes alive in the recreated scenes from the dramatic history of the past.

Seeing these remarkably preserved buildings including the barracks museum, the officer's quarters, the Mackinac museum, the guard house and the blockhouses gives one a greater understanding of the important role of Fort Mackinac in the development of the Old Northwest. The guardian guns, now silent, still protect the Citadel of the Lakes."

-Official Guide of Mackinac Island, circa 1960

Living History

Fort Mackinac is more than a relic from the past, it presents a kind of living history to its visitors. With thunderous cannons, blazing muskets and rousing bugle calls, visitors to the fort experience what military life was like in the 1880s. Period costumes, historical reenactments, craft demonstrations, informational displays and authentic artifacts housed in the restored fort buildings bring to life a rich period of American history.

Fort Holmes

Mackinac Island, Mich.   Observation Tower at Fort Holmes

MANUFACTURED BY CURT TEICH & CO., CHICAGO, ILL.

"Fort Holmes: Built by the British soon after the capture of Mackinac in 1812. The British named it Fort George, after the reigning English King, George III. When Americans took possession of the Island after the war, they named it Fort Holmes, after Major Andrew Hunter Holmes, who was killed in the battle of Mackinac Island, Aug. 4, 1814, in an attempt to take the fort from the British… Fort Holmes is on the highest point on the Island, being 318 feet above the waters of Lake Huron, and 168 feet above Fort Mackinac. Numerous are the descriptions by noted travelers, of the beautiful panorama of the surrounding waters, islands, and adjacent shores, centering about this spot. At one time there was an observatory, some seventy feet high, on its summit; but the occurrence of a serious accident in 1908, in which a life was lost, caused its removal."

-Michigan Historical Commission, *Names of Places of Interest on Mackinac Island,* 1916

OLD FORT ON HIGHEST POINT OF MACKINAC ISLAND, MICH.

Island Fathers and Heroes Sleep Here

Fort Mackinac, Mich.   U. S. Post Cemetery

"In Mackinac's old cemeteries lie many of the men and women who built homes in the new world, who helped mold the future of Mackinac and the Northwest territory, and who built for themselves a lasting monument of fame and respect… Among the hundreds interred in the old cemeteries on the hill are many names that were at one time important in Mackinac history. They founded communities, built churches and schools and homes in the new world. Soldiers of wars long since past rest quietly on the hill – some known, some unknown."

-*Mackinac Island News,* July 17, 1943

Unveiling Fr. Marquette Statue, Sept. 1st., 1909, Mackinac Island, Mich.

The honor of your presence
is requested at the unveiling ceremonies of the
statue of

PÈRE MARQUETTE,

designed by Signor Trentanove, and erected by the
Mackinac Island State Park Commission,
on Mackinac Island, Michigan.
Wednesday, September the first,
nineteen hundred and nine,
at three o'clock P.M.

Please direct reply to B. F. Emery, Supt.,
Mackinac Island, Mich.

Marquette Statue in Beauty Setting

"Marquette Park, located near the dock…always has an appeal for the visitor. With its background the white ramparts of old Fort Mackinac, its winding trails and smooth green sod, marked by shrubs and beds of bright flowers, the park has a charm beyond that of its historic association.

In the center of the Marquette Park stands a large statue of Father Jacques Marquette, the beloved Jesuit who labored among the Indians of the Northwest. The statue, by G. Trentanove of France, was a gift to Mackinac Island from Michigan school children under the leadership of Peter White of Marquette…

Father Marquette was more than a priest. He was an explorer and a pioneer. His name, taken by a railroad, a college, and by cities, villages and counties in many states, reveals in steadfast faith, the unswerving devotion and staunch courage of the Jesuits."

-Mackinac Island News, August 8, 1942

Old John Jacob Astor House, Mackinac Island, Mich.

Excellent Hotel Service

"First-class hotels are abundant at Mackinac Island; they are of all sizes and styles and prices. The oldest of them, the John Jacob Astor House, was originally the headquarters of the American Fur Co. The admirer of the antique will be well satisfied with its low ceilings, its bracing of heavy timbers, its ancient fireplaces, clumsy iron door locks, and its old storage vaults, and to cap it all, the proprietor will show the Astor account books of nearly a century ago, with their quaint entries. Located on the lake front, within a short distance of the wharf of the Detroit & Cleveland Navigation Company, are the Chippewa, the New Mackinac, the Lake View and New Murray, neat, well-appointed hostelries, liberally patronized by transients, with whom they are very popular. At the other end of the island is the Mission House, from which a fine view may be obtained. This is one of the relics, and is very popular with those seeking rest and repose."

-D & C Navigation Co., *Mackinac Island, Detroit, Cleveland, Buffalo et. al.*, circa 1908

Postcard message:

Beautiful 4th
" *Boat*
" *Food*
" *People*
" *Babies*
" *Hats!!!*
" *Feelings*
" *Comfort*
" *Conveniences*
" *Lake*
" *Views*
" *Colors*

With Love, Frances

Postmarked Mackinac Island, 1909
Mailed to Rock Island, Illinois

The Old Mission House, Mackinac Island, Mich.

Mackinac Island, Mich.   260 Island House

Mackinac Island, Mich.   253 Lake View Hotel

MANUFACTURED BY CURT TEICH & CO., CHICAGO, ILL.

Island House

"Situated in the Finest Residential Part of Mackinac Island. An ideal climate, a charming spot, novel and unsurpassed natural beauty, abundant opportunities for outdoor sports and recreation, splendid sailing and fishing, all unite in making Mackinac the most attractive summer resort of the Lakes. Golf Links, Tennis Courts and Baseball Grounds form part of the social pleasures of this beautiful Hotel and Resort.

On the American Plan. Competent management, excellent cuisine and service, and all modern improvements. Telegraph connections to all parts of the world. Long Distance telephone. A splendid orchestra in connection with Hotel, Hops in Casino three times a week. Rates $2.50 to $5.00 per day. Special Weekly rates."

-The Island House, circa 1905

133

Chippewa Hotel

"Overlooking the beautiful Straits of Mackinac, and in full view of the arrival and departure of the finest passenger steamers afloat.
OPEN JUNE TO OCTOBER.
It is our aim to make the Chippewa one of the most popular hotels on the Island, catering to first-class trade, which the appointments of the house warrant. Equipped with all modern conveniences, hot and cold water in every room, also 25 rooms with baths en suite. Broad verandas from each floor overlooking the Straits afford an ideal resting place. The Café, fronting the water, is cooled by the breezes from the lakes, making it a tempting place to dine, where you will find the best the market affords, prepared and served by competent hands.
New Addition: 25 Rooms with Bath and Pavilion with First-Class Orchestra
THE CLIMATE IS IDEAL FOR HAY FEVER SUFFERERS.
George T. Arnold, Owner and Proprietor.
Samuel S. Bradt, Manager

-Thompson, J. Russell, *J. Russell Thompson's Illustrated Souvenir Guide,* 1908

Homelike Accommodations

"The hotels which cater especially to private families are the Windsor, Palmer, The Chicago, The Iroquois, The Lake View House, and the Old Homestead. At these places home-like accommodations are given for very reasonable rates. There are also many boardinghouses at Mackinac where good accommodations are to be had for $10 to $14 per week."

-D & C Navigation Co., *Mackinac Island, Detroit, Cleveland, Buffalo et. al.*, circa 1908

IROQUOIS-ON-THE-BEACH, MACKINAC ISLAND, MICH.

Postcard message:

The big hotel on the Island is the Grand Hotel, but it is too expensive and anyway we prefer this place. It is more homelike and the meals are very good. From our room on the third floor we can see the boats coming and going.

–James

Postcard not mailed.

The New Mackinac
100 Good Rooms

"This house is well arranged for the comfort of tourists, and is conveniently located on the Lake Front, and 100 feet from the D. & C. S. N. Co.'s passenger wharf. The furniture, carpets, etc. are all NEW. The house is equipped with electric bells… gas, electricity, hot and cold water, laundry, telegraph, restaurant, fire alarm, bar-room, billiard table, sewing machine, piano, and all modern conveniences in every room… The hotel was built for the special comfort of summer boarders."

-Pleasure's Pathways, Michigan's Popular Resorts, circa 1891

PLANK'S GRAND HOTEL, MACKINAC ISLAND,

Plank's Grand Hotel

"With the construction of this noble building, Mackinac entered upon a new epoch in her history... The 'Grand' naturally constitutes the focal point of the delightful social events which follow each other rapidly during the season. In the spacious corridors and along the magnificent reach of the piazza, the man of the world will find acquaintances from all portions of the United States...

The hotel was built by a wealthy company during the spring of 1887. The plans contemplated an expenditure of $300,000, and a total capacity for 1,000 guests...

The 'Grand' is located on a high bluff on the westerly end of the island, directly overlooking the Straits of Mackinac, whence comes an almost uninterrupted Lake Michigan breeze. It is the first object discernable on board incoming steamers. The descent from the bluff to the beach is about 300 feet, accomplished easily by a rustic stair.

The rates, except for parlors, are from $3.00 to $4.00 per day, according to location of apartments."

-D & C Navigation Co., *Lake Tours via the D & C to Picturesque Mackinac*, 1890

The Grand Hotel - The Most Fashionable Resort

"This tremendous building is 650 feet in length and five stories in height. Its architecture is of the 'Old Colonial' style, the distinctive feature being a colonnaded portico, 30 feet wide, upon which the windows of every floor open. The interior is well arranged and fully equal to every demand of the most fastidious taste. The lower floor is occupied exclusively by the dining-hall, drawing-room and private parlors, with a large rotunda office in the center. The dining-hall is a mammoth apartment, capable of seating 600 people. It occupies the space of two stories, the vaulted ceiling being 27 feet overhead. The guest rooms are large, light and airy. Each front suite is provided with a private balcony. The hotel is lighted by gas and electricity, heated by steam, and provided with elevator and electric call and fire alarms. It is also supplied with a barber shop, bath-rooms, steam laundry and a first-class livery. A metropolitan orchestra is in constant attendance. The grounds have been made very attractive and a casino is constructed for indoor sports."

-Pleasures Pathways: Michigan's Popular Resorts, circa 1891

Chas. L. Fischer and his Grand Hotel Orchestra of Kalamazoo, Mich.

At Mackinac Island, Mich. 1923-4

Recreation on the Island

"Recreation is not limited to walking and sight-seeing. Two of the sportiest, best-kept and most beautiful golf courses in northern Michigan invite the golf enthusiast. Good saddle horses are available and the enticing bridle trails through the woods are numerous. There are tennis courts, baseball grounds, good bathing beaches, large outdoor swimming pools, canoes in the quiet bays of the great lakes, motorboats and sailboats. Moonlight cruises around the Island are arranged at frequent intervals.

For the younger set and those who enjoy society, entertainment is provided by dances given at the hotels every evening and the afternoon dancing in the Tea Garden at the Grand Hotel."

-Mackinac Island Michigan, circa 1920

Postcard message:

Dear Mary Louise,
This is a delightful place for relaxation; also quite primitive; no trains, no cars, only carriages and bicycles. We are located in a lovely home in the center of the village and have a room overlooking the water. We go to sleep and waken to the rhythmatic thud of horses' hooves. We have walked around the Island – 7 miles. Can really use the stock expression "wish you were here with us."
Love, Lillian

Postmarked Mackinac Island, 1928
Mailed to Springfield, Ohio

SWIMMING POOL AND AFTERNOON TEA GARDEN, GRAND HOTEL, MACKINAC ISLAND, MICH.

Grand Hotel Golf Links

"The golf course at the Grand Hotel is in excellent shape. The turf is rich and lush, greens are undulating, yet true and with many of the hazards stiffened, the course offers a challenge to any golfer seeking par."

-Mackinac Island News, June 25, 1938

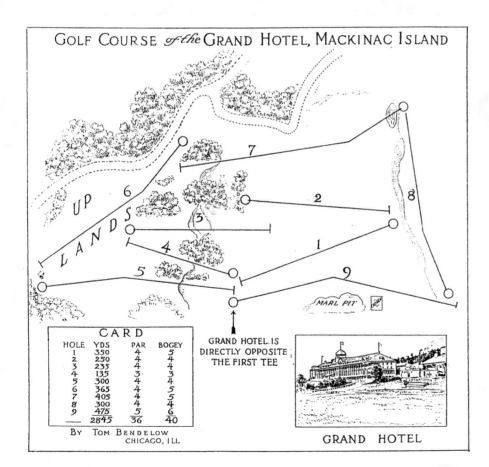

Postcard message:

Hi!
Beautiful day – just came from steamship excursion & are going on a carriage tour tomorrow. Played golf yesterday. The gang's all here. Had speedboat ride by moonlight – ah!

Love, M.

Postmarked Mackinac Island, 1929
Mailed to Newago, Mich.

Grand Hotel Golf Links, Mackinac Island, Mich.

Magnificent Summer Cottages

    Mackinac Island is well known for its magnificent summer homes. The Windermere, meaning "wind from the lake", is an example of one of the Island's truly splendid summer "cottages." The Anthony brothers built the cottage on Biddle Point in 1877. It is the earliest example of the Queen Anne style on the Island. The unique tower was the cottage's most distinctive feature. From its large windows, cottagers could watch the steady stream of boats coming and going in the Island's harbor. Mr. and Mrs. Patrick Doud purchased the cottage in 1906 and converted it into a hotel, which continued to be operated by the family for over a century. It was remodeled several times, the tower was dismantled; today the structure bears little resemblance to its original form.

Peaceful Cottage Life

"…Bigness, coolness, keen sweeping winds, a view of the broad Straits and far away down Lake Michigan, from every one of the high, wide windows, soft, cool colors and clear spaces are seen, while inside, restful to the eye, a few quiet toned pictures, billowy cushions in dainty tints just where you want them, not too many draperies, natural wood finishings, sleeping apartments as large as the drawing room at home, unexpected little alcoves everywhere, fitted with sleep enticing couches, verandas with hammocks swung across the corners, the cool shadows and deep stillness of the woods just at the back door, the broad shimmering, ever-changing glory of the blue lake in front – this is a Mackinac cottage! One never wonders, who has seen them, why it is that the summer resident holds his cottage on Mackinac Heights as the crown of his possessions…"

-Petoskey Evening News & Daily Resorter, July 28, 1894

Interior view of the main living area of "Casa Verano," the summer home of the Delos and Daisy Blodgett family of Grand Rapids. Located on the West Bluff, the cottage was built in 1893.

TERRACE COTTAGE

MACKINAC ISLAND   MICHIGAN

P. KERRIGAN, PROPRIETOR

Perfect Refuge

"Mackinac Island is…a refuge for the over tasked brains and bodies of St. Louis and Chicago citizens, who, being always wide awake at home, need the perfect repose furnished at Mackinac, where, unvexed by daily mail or telegram, they can fill their lungs with oxygen and their stomachs with whitefish."

-Clarke, S. "Mackinaw," Putnam's Magazine, July 1868

Summer Cottages Worth $50,000

"Even in antebellum times Mackinac Island was famous during the summer season as the temporary home of wealthy and aristocratic society…where they spent the summer season on the delightful bluffs overlooking the straits… The palatial residences of the merchant prince, the banker and the captain of industry now fill every available place on the edge of the broad plateau overlooking the harbor. Here are summer cottages worth $50,000, where during the season some of the men most distinguished in politics and trade make their home with their families."

-*Grand Rapids Herald,* June 26, 1904

CHICAGO STREET AND GRAND HOTEL, MACKINAC ISLAND, MICH.

Hundreds of Cottages

"Several hundred beautiful summer homes have been built by people from all parts of the country, who make Mackinac their permanent summer residence. Many desirable sites are still available. Completely furnished cottages may be rented for $200 to $1,000 a season."

-*Mackinac Island, Michigan*, circa 1920

Postcard message:

Dear Folks:-
Arrived safe and well — was an ideal trip on the water and all enjoyed it. Hope you are well and not baked in Chicago. We are settled in with Aunt and Uncle in their summer home on the Island. Such a lovely place. Will write more — Love to you all from all of us.

-The Randolphs

Postmarked Mackinac Island, 1916
Mailed to Chicago, Illinois

Cottages on Lake Front.   MACKINAC ISLAND, Mich.

The Young Cottage

"Since last summer, Mr. Young has had an elegant new cottage built, just west of the Fort, at the top of the bluff overlooking the village and harbor. It is an ideal spot, giving a beautiful view of the water for many miles around, as well as of the town. The cottage itself is one of the most beautiful ones on the Island, with an immense veranda extending across the front of it and running back some distance on each side. Within, it is very elegantly furnished, and when fully completed in a few days, will make an exceedingly beautiful and elegant summer home…"

-Petoskey Evening News and Daily Resorter,
July 1, 1902

The Governor's Summer Residence

Lawrence and Mabel Young, a wealthy couple from Chicago, completed this beautiful Shingle Style/Arts and Crafts cottage in 1902 on the "West Fort Lot" leased from the Mackinac Island State Park Commission. In 1926 the cottage was sold to Hugo and Clara Scherer of Detroit, who, in turn, sold it to the State of Michigan in 1945 for use as the official summer residence of the governor of Michigan. The State paid the Scherer family $15,000 for the cottage, which was the same amount the Youngs paid for its construction.

9849 SUNSET ON THE "STRAITS", MACKINAC ISLAND, MICH.

Postcard message:

It's so beautiful here! Almost a dream world. Wish we could stay all summer. Are having the time of our lives.

- Chris and Tom

Postmarked Mackinac Island, 1912
Mailed to Pontiac, Mich.

Bibliography & Sources Cited
Sources cited in text are asterisked.

Books, Periodicals, Serials, Pamphlets, and Brochures

Armour, David A. 100 Years at Mackinac: A Centennial History of the Mackinac Island State Park *Commission, 1895-1995*. [Mackinac Island, Mich.: Mackinac State Historic Parks, 1995].

Bailey, John R. *Mackinac, Formerly Michilimackinac; A History and Guide Book, with Maps*. Grand Rapids, Mich.: Tradesman Company, 1909.

*Baird, Willard. *Modern Miracle: A Series of Articles Concerning the Mackinac Straits Bridge*. [Sault Ste. Marie, Mich.]: Federated Publications, Inc., 1952.

Benjamin, Robert E. *Mackinac Island: An Illustrated History, Guide and Map of the Straits of Michilimackinac*. Mackinac Island, Mich.: Benjamin's Photo Art Service, [1951].

----------. *Mackinac Island: Three Hundred Years of History*. [Mackinac Island, Mich.: Benjamin of Mackinac Island, 1955].

Brisson, Steven C. *Wish You Were Here: An Album of Vintage Mackinac Postcards*. Mackinac Island, Mich.: Mackinac State Historical Parks, [2002].

Brown, Prentiss Marsh. *The Mackinac Bridge Story*. Detroit, Mich.: Wayne University Press, 1956.

Brown, Robert. *Passenger Travel on the Great Lakes*. Grand Marais, Mich.: Voyager Press, 1978.

Chicago, Duluth & Georgian Bay Transit Co., *Pleasure Cruises for Leisure Days*. N.p.: n.p., [1935].

----------., *A Week's Cruise on Four Lakes - Season 1923*. Chicago: General Printing Co., 1923.

Chippewa Totem Village, N.p.: n.p., [1960].

Cisler, Walker Lee. *Michigan's Giant Stride: The Story of the Mackinac Bridge*. New York: Newcomen Society in North America, 1967.

City of St. Ignace: And Its Surroundings, Its Attractions for Tourist, Health Seeker, Historian, Traveler, and Visitor. St. Ignace, Mich.: Business Men's Association, 1901.

City of St. Ignace and Mackinac County, for the Year 1895: [St. Ignace, Mich.]: E. Jones, 1895.

Clarke, S. "Mackinaw," *Putnam's Magazine*, July 1868.

Cloverland Tourist's Guide. Menominee, Mich.: Herald-Leader Pub. Co, 1931-1932.

Detroit and Cleveland Navigation Company. *The Grand Fleet of the Great Lakes: Detroit, Cleveland, Buffalo, Niagara Falls, Mackinac Island, St. Ignace, Chicago*. [Detroit, Mich.: Detroit and Cleveland Navigation Co.], 1936.

------------. *Hunting and Fishing Resorts of the Great Lakes via Picturesque Mackinac*. Buffalo, N.Y.: Matthews & Northrup Co., 1887.

------------. *Lake Erie & Lake Huron*. Detroit, Mich.: O.S. Gulley, Bornman & Co., [1886].

*------------. *Lake Tours via the D & C to Picturesque Mackinac*. Detroit, Mich.: Press of John Bornman & Son, 1890.

*------------. *Mackinac Island, Detroit, Cleveland, Buffalo & Niagara Falls, Toledo, Alpena, Saginaw, Bay City, St. Clair, Port Huron, Harbor Beach, Oscoda, Cheboygan, St. Ignace*. [Detroit, Mich.: n.p., 1908].

*----------. *Midsummer Voyages on Northern Seas*. N.p.: Cleveland, Detroit and Cleveland Co., [1890].

*----------. *Pleasure Days on the Great Blue Lakes 1931*. N.p.: n.p., 1931.

----------. *Water Way Tales*. Detroit, Mich.: Detroit & Cleveland Navigation Co., [1920].

Detroit & Mackinac Railway Company. *Health & Pleasure Resorts: Inexpensive Outings & Vacations*. [Detroit, Mich.: Franklin Press, 1915].

----------. *Local Time Tables and Through Connections*. Detroit, Mich.: The Railway, 1906.

----------. *Tawas Beach: A Health Resort Among the Pine Trees of Northern Michigan Situated on Tawas Bay, Lake Huron*. Bay City, Mich.: Detroit & Mackinac Railway Co., [1903].

*Disturnell, John. *Island of Mackinac, Giving a Description of all the Objects of Interest and Places of Resort in the Straits of Mackinac and Its Vicinity*. Philadelphia: n.p., 1875.

Donan, P. *Mackinac Island, the Wave-Washed Tourists' Paradise of the Unsalted Seas*. [St. Louis: Times Print House, 1882].

*East Michigan Tourist Association. *East Michigan Tourist Guide*. Bay City, Mich.: East Michigan Tourist Association, 1930-1934.

----------. *Eastern and Central Michigan Playtime Book*. Bay City, Mich.: East Michigan Tourist Association, 1948-1949.

*----------. *Eat-Sleep-Shop in East Michigan*. Bay City, Mich.: East Michigan Tourist Association, [1940-1945].

----------. *Playtime Guide Book*. Bay City, Mich.: East Michigan Tourist Association, 1955-1959.

----------. *Your Guidebook to Eastern and Central Michigan*. Bay City, Mich.: East Michigan Tourist Association, 1945.

*Eby, C.C. *Mackinac County of the Straits Country*. [St. Ignace: C.C. Eby, 1923-1930].

Fuller, Florence. *Map and Guide of Mackinac Island*. N.p.: n.p. [1926].

Gardiner, William H. *Picturesque Mackinac: The Photographs of William H. Gardiner, 1896-1915*. Mackinac Island, Mich.: Mackinac State Historic Parks, [2005].

Goodrich Steamship Lines, on Lake Michigan and Picturesque Mackinac Island. Chicago: Goodrich Transit Co., 1920.

Grand Rapids & Indiana Railroad Company. *Golf Links on the Grand Rapids and Indiana Railway*. N.p.: Grand Rapids & Indiana Railway, [1910].

*----------. *Mackinac, the Wonderful Isle, Petoskey, Traverse City, and Other Northern Michigan Summer Resorts*. Grand Rapids, Mich.: Grand Rapids & Indiana Railroad Co., [1890-1892].

----------. *Michigan in Summer*. N.p.: n.p., 1903-1910.

----------. *Northern Michigan Lakes and Summer Resorts*. Chicago: Cameron, Amberg & Co., [1880].

Great Lakes Transit Company. *Great Lakes Cruise, Season 1919*. Chicago: Poole Bros., 1919.

Hilton, George Woodman. *The Great Lakes Car Ferries*. Berkeley, Calif.: Howell-North, 1962.

Historic Mackinac Island: Michigan's Famous Summer Resort. N.p.: n.p., [1940].

Horton, Irvin W., Georgia M Horton. *A Complete Guidebook to Michigan's Upper Peninsula*. Sault Ste. Marie, Mich.: [Horton], 1961-1962.

*Hudson, Roberts P. *Michigan: A Summer and Health Resort State*. [Lansing, Mich.: State Board of Health], 1898.

Information Bureau, St. Ignace, Michigan. *St. Ignace-Charming Summer Playground*. St. Ignace, Mich.: n.p., [1935].

Inglis, James Gale. *Northern Michigan, Handbook for Travelers*. Petoskey, Mich.: Geo. E. Sprang, 1898.

Inland Seas. Vermillion, Ohio: Great Lakes Historical Society, 1950-1960.

Inside Michigan. Detroit, Mich.: n.p., 1952-1958.

Island House, Mackinac Island. Chicago, Ill.: Press of Charles A. Taylors Company, [1905].

Island View Cabins, St. Ignace, Michigan, for the Rest of Your Life. N.p.: n.p., [1945].

Kiwanis Club. *Before the Bridge: A History and Directory of St. Ignace and Nearby Localities*. St. Ignace, Mich.: n.p., 1957.

Lake View, Mackinac Island. N.p.: n.p., [1920].

Mackinac Bridge Authority. *Mackinac Bridge: World's Greatest Bridge: Connecting Michigan's Upper and Lower Peninsulas at St. Ignace and Mackinaw City*. St. Ignace, Mich.: Mackinac Bridge Authority, [1960].

Mackinac Bridge Dedication Festival – June 26-28, 1958. N.p.: n.p., 1958.

Mackinac Island Michigan. N.p.: n.p., [1920].

*Mackinac Island State Park Commission. *Historic Fort Michilimackinac*. Lansing: Allied Printing,

[1965].

----------. *Historic Guidebook: Mackinac Island*. N.p.: Mackinac Island State Park Commission, 1962.

---------. *Mackinac History: An Informal Series of Illustrated Vignettes*. Mackinac Island, Mich.: Mackinac Island State Park Commission, 1963-1982.

Mackinac Island: The Magazine Guide. Milwaukee, Wis.: W.A. Krueger Co., [1940].

Mackinac Straits Shores: Michigan the Popular Summer Home and Playground of America. Detroit, Mich.: Pilgrim Realty Co., [1926].

Mackinac Straits Tourist Association. *Famous Straits Region of Michigan*. Sault Ste. Marie, Mich.: n.p., [1940].

Mackinac Under Three Flags: Tourist Guide and History. Mackinac Island, Mich.: Wickman's Photo & Gift Shop, 1928.

*Mackinaw City Chamber of Commerce. *Chief of All Vacation Places Invites You to Mackinaw City, Michigan*. N.p.: n.p., [1930].

*Mackinaw City Chamber of Commerce. *Stop Over at Mackinaw City*. [Cheboygan]: Al Weber's Cheboygan Observer Print, [1933-1935].

McCabe, John. *Grand Hotel, Mackinac Island*. Sault Ste. Marie, Mich.: Unicorn Press, 1987.

McCoy, Raymond. *The Massacre of Old Fort Mackinac (Michilimackinac)*. Bay City, Mich.: McCoy, [1950].

McKee, Russell. *Mackinac, The Gathering Place*. Lansing, Mich.: Michigan Natural Resources Magazine, [1981].

*Michigan Central Railroad. *The Fairy Isle of Mackinac*. N.p.: Passenger Dept., Michigan Central Railroad, [1880-1900].

----------. *The Island of Mackinac: (U.S. National Park)*. [Detroit, Mich.: Michigan Central Railroad, 1886].

*----------. *Michigan Resorts, Chiefly in Northern Michigan*. N.p.: Michigan Central Railroad Co., [1900].

----------. *Summer in Michigan*. N.p.: Michigan Central Railroad, 1917-1932.

*----------. *Summer Vacation Tours*. N.p.: Michigan Central Railroad, 1910.

Michigan Dept. of Conservation, Parks and Recreation Division. *Straits State Park*. Lansing, Mich.: Michigan Dept of Conservation, Parks and Recreation Division, [1950].

*Michigan Historical Commission. *Names of Places of Interest on Mackinac Island, Michigan*. Lansing, Mich.: Wynkoop, Hallenbeck, Crawford Co., State Printers, 1916.

Michigan History Magazine. Lansing, Mich.: Bureau of History, Michigan Department of State., 1980-2006.

Michigan Magazine. Petoskey, Mich.: Heirs of C.E. Kimball, 1930.

*Michigan State Highway Department. *Michigan Official Highway Map*. Lansing, Mich.: Michigan State Highway Dept., 1958.

----------. *Michigan State Ferries Year 'round Service Schedule*. [Mich.]: Michigan State Highway Department, 1939-1940.

*----------. *Michigan State Ferry Schedule*. [Mich.]: Michigan State Highway Department, 1946-1957.

Michigan Tradesman. Grand Rapids, Mich.: Tradesman Co., 1940-1958.

*Michigan Transit Company. *Vacation Lake Trips -"Just Long Enough"*. N.p.: n.p., 1928-1930.

Michilimackinac Historical Society. *Michilimackinac. Commemorating the Opening of the Mackinac Bridge (Dedication Festival, June 26-28,1958)*. St. Ignace, Mich.: Mackinac County Chamber of Commerce, 1958.

Michilimackinac Historical Society. *St. Ignace: Over 300 Years of History*. St. Ignace, Mich.: Michilimackinac Historical Society, [1975].

Mystery Spot – St. Ignace, Michigan. N.p.: n.p., [1953].

Newnom, Clyde L. *Michigan's Thirty-Seven Million Acres of Diamonds*. Detroit, Mich.: The Book of Michigan Company, 1927.

Newton, Stan. *Mackinac Island and Sault Ste. Marie: Picturesque and Legendary*. Grand Rapids, Mich.: Black Letter Press, 1976.

Northern Michigan Magazine. Petoskey, Mich.: C.E. Kimball, 1926-1929.

Official Carriage Tour of Mackinac Island. N.p.: n.p., [1950].

Official Guide of Mackinac Island. N.p.: n.p., [1960].

Official Mackinac Bridge Souvenir Book: Dedication Festival June 26th, 27th, 28th, 1958. Detroit, Mich.: Mackinac Bridge Dedication Festival Committee, 1958.

Olson, David J. *The Mackinac Bridge*. Lansing, Mich.: Michigan History Division, Michigan Department of State, [1985].

Owen Sound Transportation Company. *The Famous Mackinac Cruise via Georgian Bay and Manitoulin Island*. N.p.: n.p., [1930].

Petersen, Eugene T. *Guide Book for Mackinac Island Visitors*. [Michigan]: Mackinac Island State Park Commission, [1979].

----------. *Inside Mackinac*. St. Ignace, Mich.: Inside Mackinac, [1990].

----------. *Mackinac in Restoration*. [Lansing, Mich.]: Mackinac Island State Park Commission, [1983].

----------. *Mackinac Island: Its History in Pictures*. Mackinac Island, Mich.: Mackinac Island State Park Commission, [1973].

----------. *Mackinac's Grand Hotel: The Early Years*. Ann Arbor, Mich.: Historical Society of Michigan, [1988].

----------. *Michilimackinac: Its History and Restoration*. Mackinac Island, Mich.: Fort Mackinac Division Press, 1962.

----------. *The Preservation of History at Mackinac*. [Lansing, Mich.]: Mackinac Island State Park Commission, [1972].

Piljac, Thomas M., and Pamela Lach. *Mackinac Island: Historic Frontier, Vacation Resort, Timeless Wonderland*. Chicago, Ill.: Chicago Review Press, 1996.

Pleasure's Pathway: Michigan's Popular Resorts. Olivet, Mich.: Wever & Obenauer, [1891].

*Polk, R.L. & Co. *Michigan State Gazetteer and Business Directory*. Detroit: R.L. Polk & Co., 1871-1931/32.

Porter, Phil. *Fudge: Mackinac's Sweet Souvenir*. Mackinac Island, Mich.: Mackinac State Historic Parks, [2001].

----------. *Mackinac: An Island Famous in These Regions*. Mackinac Island, Mich.: Mackinac State Historic Parks, [1998].

----------. *View from the Veranda: The History and Architecture of the Summer Cottages on Mackinac Island*. Mackinac Island, Mich.: Mackinac Island State Park Commission, [2006].

Ranville, Judy. *Memories of Mackinaw: A Bicentennial Project of Mackinaw City Public Library & Mackinaw City Woman's Club*. [Mackinaw City, Mich.: Mackinaw City Public Library, 1976].

Ratigan, William. *Straits of Mackinac! Crossroads of the Great Lakes*. Grand Rapids, Mich.: Eerdmans, [1957].

Recognized Tourist Cabin Camp Guide. N.p.: n.p., 1938-1941.

*Robinson, George. *History of Cheboygan and Mackinac Counties*. [Cheboygan, Mich.]: G. Robinson, 1873.

Rogers, Frank Foster. *History of the Michigan State Highway Department, 1905-1933*. Lansing, Mich.: [Franklin DeKleine Company, printers and binders], 1933.

Rubin, Lawrence A. *Bridging the Straits: The Story of Mighty Mac*. Detroit: Wayne State University Press, [1985].

Sculle, Keith. "Castle Rock in the Eby Family Tradition," *Chronicle*, Spring 2006, 8-10.

Selected Scenes of Mackinac Island-Hand Colored. N.p.: n.p. [1910].

Smith, Gregg. *The Mackinac Bridge Story*. Bay City, Mich.: Souvenir Book Co., 1957.

Souvenir of Mackinac Island. Chicago: Happy Hill, [1900].

Souvenir Program of St. Ignace 300th Birthday and Pere Marquette Pageant, 1671-1971. St. Ignace, Mich.: Father Marquette Historical Production Association, [1971].

*Stace, Arthur William. *Touring the Coasts of Michigan*. Ann Arbor, Mich.: Booth Newspapers, 1937-1938.

Standard Guide, Mackinac Island and Northern Lake Resorts. N.p.: Foster & Reynolds, 1904.

Steinman, David Barnard. *The Mackinac Bridge: Conquering the Impossible*. Boston: Boston Society of Civil Engineers, 1956.

----------. *Miracle Bridge at Mackinac*. Grand Rapids, Mich.: Eerdmans, [1957].

St. Ignace Area: Historic, Magnificent, Beautiful. Saint Ignace, Mich.: St. Ignace Area Chamber of Commerce, [1960].

*St. Ignace Information Bureau. *Gateway to Hiawatha-Land*. St. Ignace, Mich.: n.p., [1930].

Stites, Susan, and Lea Ann Sterling, *Historic Cottages of Mackinac Island*. Mayfield, Mich.: Arbutus Press, [2001].

*Thomson, J. Russell. *J. Russell Thomson's Illustrated Souvenir Guide, Northern Michigan Resorts*. Grand Rapids, Mich.: Northern Michigan Guide Book Co., 1906-1908.

Traverse, the Magazine. [Traverse City, Mich.]: Prism Publication, 1990-2006.

Treasure Island, St. Ignace, Mich.: N.p.: n.p., [1960].

*United States Railroad Administration. *Michigan Summer Resorts*. [Washington, D.C.]: United States Railroad Administration, [1920].

Upper Michigan Ahoy Vacationist. N.p.: n.p., [1930].

*Upper Peninsula Development Bureau. *Cloverland: The Tourist's Paradise*. [Marquette, Mich.]: Upper Peninsula Development Bureau, [1925].

----------. *Cloverland, Upper Peninsula of Michigan: The Tourist's Paradise*. [Marquette, Mich.]: Upper Peninsula Development Bureau, [1930].

*----------. *The Land of Hiawatha: Upper Peninsula of Michigan*. Marquette, Mich.: Upper Peninsula Development Bureau, 1928-1934.

*----------. *The Lure Book of Michigan's Upper Peninsula*. Marquette, Mich.: Upper Peninsula Development Bureau, 1939-1952.

----------. *Lured by the land of Hiawatha*. Marquette, Mich.: Upper Peninsula Development Bureau, 1938.

*----------. *The Lure of Michigan's Upper Peninsula*. Marquette, Mich.: Upper Peninsula Development Bureau, 1953-1958.

----------. *The Lure of the Land of Hiawatha: Michigan's Upper Peninsula*. Marquette, Mich.: Upper Peninsula Development Bureau, 1935-1937.

Vacation in St. Ignace: Hub of the Historic Straits Region. N.p.: n.p., [1945].

Van Fleet, James Alvin. *Summer Resorts of the Mackinaw Region, and Adjacent Localities*. [Detroit, Mich.: Lever Press, 1882].

Views of Mackinac Island. [Portland, ME.: Chisholm Bros., 1900].

Visitors Bureau, St. Ignace. *St. Ignace-Charming Summer Playground*. N.p.: n.p., [1940].

Wallace, E. W. *Pictorial Mackinac Island: (formerly Michilimackinac)*. Mackinac Island, Mich.: E.W. Wallace, [1907].

*West Michigan Pike Association. *Maps, Routes and Tourist Directory of the West Michigan Pike*. [Muskegon, Mich.]: West Michigan Pike Association, 1915.

*West Michigan Tourist and Resort Association. *Carefree Days in West Michigan*. Grand Rapids, Mich.: West Michigan Tourist and Resort Association, 1940-1960.

Why? Go Elsewhere for Rest or Vacation: Stay in Mackinac County. [St. Ignace, Mich.]: Mackinac Conservation Club, [1953].

Widder, Keith R. *Mackinac National Park, 1875-1895*. [Lansing, Mich.]: Mackinac Island State Park Commission, [1975].

Williams, Meade C. *Early Mackinac. A Sketch, Historical and Descriptive*. New York: Duffield & Co., 1919.

Wood, Edwin Orin. *Historic Mackinac; the Historical, Picturesque and Legendary Features of the Mackinac Country*. New York: The Macmillan Company, 1918.

Woodfill, W. Stewart. *Grand Hotel; the Story of an Institution*. New York: Newcomen Society in North America, 1969.

*Writers' Program of the Work Projects Administration in the State of Michigan. *Michigan; a Guide to the Wolverine state*. New York: Oxford University Press, [1941].

Newspapers

Cheboygan Daily Tribune
Detroit Times
Emmet County Graphic
Grand Rapids Herald
Grand Rapids Press
Holland Evening Sentinel
Island News
Mackinac Island News
Mackinac Island Town Crier
Mackinac Islander
Petoskey Evening News
Republican-News
Republican-News and St. Ignace Enterprise
St. Ignace Enterprise
Traverse City Record-Eagle

Special Collections

Archives of Michigan, Michigan Historical Center

Bentley Historical Library, University of Michigan

Clarke Historical Library, Central Michigan University

Curt Teich Postcard Archives, Lake County (IL) Discovery Museum

Grand Rapids History & Special Collections, Grand Rapids Public Library

Illustration Credits

We are grateful to the following institutions and individuals for allowing us the use of r images.

Front cover Teyson Photography; **Back cover** Archives of Michigan, hand-colored by nne Carroll Burdick; **Title page** St. Ignace Chamber of Commerce, *Michigan's Mackinac nty Upper Peninsula Gem,* circa 1960; **Verso:** Mackinac Straits Tourist Association, *The Famous its Region of Michigan,* circa 1940: **vi** Lake County (IL) Discovery Museum, Curt Teich card Archives; **vii** G. H. Wickman; **viii** Archives of Michigan; **1** Mackinac Straits Tourist ociation, *The Famous Straits Region of Michigan,* circa 1940; **2** Detroit & Cleveland Navigation Hunting and Fishing Resorts of the Great Lakes, circa 1887, from the Clarke Historical Library, ral Michigan University; **3** Detroit Publishing Co.; **4** (left) Goodrich Steamship Lines, *On e Michigan and Picturesque Mackinac Island,* 1920, (middle) Great Lakes Transit Company, *Great es Cruise, Season 1919,* (right) Owen Sound Transportation Company, *The Famous Mackinac se,* circa 1930; **5** Michigan Transit Company, *Vacation Lake Trips,* 1928; **6** (left) Chicago, uth & Georgian Bay Transit Co., *A Week's Cruise on Four Lakes,* 1923, (upper right) Chicago, uth & Georgian Bay Transit Co., *Pleasure Cruises for Leisure Days,* circa 1935, (lower right) e County (IL) Discovery Museum, Curt Teich Postcard Archives; **7** (left) Detroit & eland Navigation Company, *The Grand Fleet of the Great Lakes,* 1936, (lower right) Detroit & eland Navigation Company, *Pleasure Days on the Great Blue Lakes 1931;* **9** (right) C.C. Eby, kinac County of the Straits Country, 1927; **10** (left) Grand Rapids Public Library; (middle left) nd Rapids & Indiana Railway, *Michigan Summer,* 1903, (middle right) Detroit & Mackinac way, *Local Time Tables,* 1906, (right) Detroit & Mackinac Railway, *Tawas Beach,* circa 1903, n the Clarke Historical Library, Central Michigan University; **11** (upper left) Michigan ral Railroad, *Summer in Michigan,* 1930, (right) Michigan Central Railroad, *Mackinac Island Michigan Resorts,* 1930, Library of Michigan, an agency of the Department of History, Arts Libraries; **12** (right) Boyne City Historical Commission; **13** (right) *Mackinac Straits Shores,* 1926, from the Clarke Historical Library, Central Michigan University; **14** G-I Holdings, **17** Mackinaw City Chamber of Commerce, *Stop Over at Mackinaw City,* circa 1935; **20** Lake nty (IL) Discovery Museum, Curt Teich Postcard Archives; **22** (upper right) *Michigan teer,* 1917; **23** (postcards) G-I Holdings, (ad) West Michigan Tourist Association, *Carefree in West Michigan,* 1949; **24** G-I Holdings; **25** (ad) East Michigan Tourist Association, *East igan Tourist Guide,* 1932; **26** (ad) East Michigan Tourist Association, *Eastern & Central igan Playtime,* 1948; **29** G-I Holdings; **31** (lower) G-I Holdings; **32** (upper) Lake County (IL) overy Museum, Curt Teich Postcard Archives; (lower) East Michigan Tourist Association, *Michigan Tourist Guide,* 1932; **33** Lake County (IL) Discovery Museum, Curt Teich Postcard ives; **34** (lower) G-I Holdings; **35** Lake County (IL) Discovery Museum, Curt Teich card Archives; **37** (upper right) Don Geske family, (lower right) Johnson Studios, oygan; **39** Archives of Michigan; **40** (ad) *Michigan Gazetteer,* 1907; **42** (left) Johnson Studio, oygan; **43** *Michigan Magazine* Aug/Sept. 1930; **44** Michigan State Highway Department, *igan State Ferries Year 'Round Service Schedule,* 1939; **45** Sam McIntire visual materials series, ley Historical Library, University of Michigan; **47** (upper) Johnson Studios, Cheboygan; **49** er) Archives of Michigan; **50** (upper) G-I Holdings; **51** Lake County (IL) Discovery um, Curt Teich Postcard Archives; **52** (upper) Grand Rapids Public Library, (lower) ives of Michigan; **53** (left) Lake County (IL) Discover Museum, Curt Teich Postcard ives, (upper right & middle) Michigan State Highway Department, *Michigan State Ferry ule,* 1954, (lower right) Don Geske family; **54** Archives of Michigan; **55** (left two items) Geske family, (right) United Press International photo from the G. Mennen Williams l materials series, Bentley Historical Library, University of Michigan; **56** G-I Holdings; **57**

Mackinac Bridge Authority, *Mackinac Bridge: World's Greatest Bridge,* circa 1960; **58** copyright, Penrod-Hiawatha; **59-60** Archives of Michigan; **61** Superior View/Jack Deo; **62** (upper & lower) copyright, Penrod-Hiawatha, (middle) Don Geske family; **63** Grand Rapids Public Library; **64** Archives of Michigan; **65** (upper right) Archives of Michigan, (lower right) Mackinac Bridge Authority/Don Geske family; **66** (left) Don Geske family; **67** (upper right) Don Geske family, (middle) Archives of Michigan; **68** (left) Don Geske family, (right) Archives of Michigan; **69** (upper left) G-I Holdings, (right) Archives of Michigan / Don Geske family; **70** (upper left) Superior View/Jack Deo, (lower left) *Official Mackinac Bridge Souvenir Book,* 1958, (right) H.J. Bell, St. Ignace; **71** (left) Michigan Tourist Council, (right) West Michigan Tourist Association, *Carefree Days in West Michigan,* 1958; **72** G-I Holdings; **73** C.C. Eby, *Mackinac County of the Straits Country,* 1927; **74** (left) Detroit Publishing Co., (right) Hugh Leighton Co.; **75** (left) J.J. Soucie, St. Ignace, (right) V.O. Hammon Pub. Co.; **76** V.O. Hammon Pub. Co.; **77** (left) C.C. Eby, *Mackinac County of the Straits Country,* circa 1925; **78** (postcards) Mulcrones Bazaar, St. Ignace, (ad) *Michigan Gazetteer,* 1891; **79** (upper & Lower) C.C. Eby, (middle) C.C. Eby, *Mackinac County of the Straits Country,* 1927; **80** (postcards) Artvue Post Card Co., N.Y., (ad) Upper Peninsula Development Bureau, *The Lure Book of Michigan's Upper Peninsula,* 1945; **81** (ad) Upper Peninsula Development Bureau, *Lured by the Land of Hiawatha,* 1938, (postcards) Dexter Press, Pearl River, N.Y.; **82** C.C. Eby, *Mackinac County of the Straits Country,* circa 1926 from the Clarke Historical Library, Central Michigan University; **83** (upper left) Upper Peninsula Development Bureau, *The Lure Book of Michigan's Upper Peninsula,* 1945, (middle left) G-I Holdings, ((lower right) Home Service Studios, Manistee; **84** (upper left) G-I Holdings, (lower left & right) *Island View Cabins - St. Ignace, Michigan,* circa 1945; **85** (postcards) G-I holdings, (ad) Kiwanis Club, St. Ignace, Mich., *Before the Bridge,* 1957; **86** (upper) C.C. Eby, (lower) C.C. Eby, *Mackinac County of the Straits Country,* circa 1926, from the Bentley Historical Library, University of Michigan; **87** (lower) Upper Peninsula Development Bureau, *Lure of the Land of Hiawatha,* circa 1936; **88** (postcards) G-I Holdings, (ad) Upper Peninsula Development Bureau, *The Lure Book of Michigan's Upper Peninsula,* 1947; **89** (postcards) G-I Holdings, (ad) Upper Peninsula Development Bureau, *Lure of the Land of Hiawatha,* 1936; **91** Visitors Bureau, St. Ignace, *St. Ignace - Charming Summer Playground,* circa 1940; **92** Albertype Co., N.Y.; **93** (left) Lake County (IL) Discovery Museum, Curt Teich Postcard Archives, (right lower) Mackinac Conservation Club, *Why? Go Elsewhere for Vacation,* 1953; **94** (upper left) Lake County (IL) Discovery Museum, Curt Teich Postcard Archives, (ad) Upper Peninsula Development Bureau, *Lure of the Land of Hiawatha,* circa 1935, (lower right) C. C. Eby; **95** (upper) C.C. Eby, (lower left) C.C. Eby, *Mackinac County of the Straits Country,* 1927; **96** (postcards) Albertype Co., N.Y., *(ad) Cloverland Tourist Guide,* 1929; **97** G-I Holdings; **98** (left) Michigan Department of Conservation, *Straits State Park,* circa 1950, (right) Archives of Michigan; **99** (postcards) G-I Holdings, (ad) Irvin and Georgia Horton, *Complete Guidebook to Michigan's Upper Peninsula,* 1961; **100** (upper) Tichnor Bros., Boston, (lower) G-I Holdings; **101** (left) Totem Village, *Chippewa Totem Village,* (postcard) Freeman Studios, Berrien Springs; **104** (left) *Views of Mackinac* circa 1900, from the Clarke Historical Library, Central Michigan University, (right) Superior View/Jack Deo; **105** (left) J. Disturnell, *Island of Mackinac and Its Vicinity,* 1875 from the Clarke Historical Library, Central Michigan University, (middle) *Souvenir of Mackinac Island,* circa 1900, Grand Rapids Public Library, (right) *Standard Guide to Mackinac Island,* 1904; **106** (left) Archives of Michigan, (right) J. Disturnell, *Island of Mackinac and Its Vicinity,* 1875, from the Bentley Historical Library, University of Michigan; **107** Mackinac Island, Michigan visual materials collection, Bentley Historical Library, University of Michigan; **108** P.B. Greene photographic collection, Bentley Historical Library, University of Michigan; **109** Clarke Historical Library, Central Michigan University; **110** *Mackinac Island* circa 1920, from the Clarke Historical Library, Central Michigan University; **111** (right) G. H.W.; **113** (left) East Michigan Tourist Association, *East Michigan Tourist Guide,* 1931, (right) Lake County (IL) Discovery Museum, Curt Teich Postcard Archives; **114** *Selected Scenes of Mackinac of Island Hand*

Colored, circa 1910; **115** V.O. Hammon Pub. Co.; **116** (left) Edward Drier photograph collection, Bentley Historical Library, University of Michigan, (right) Grand Hotel/Rose Photos from the Emil Lorch photograph series, Bentley Historical Library, University of Michigan, (ad) *Island News,* Sept. 8, 1949; **117** Grand Hotel/Rose Photos from the Emil Lorch photograph series, Bentley Historical Library, University of Michigan; **119** (left) Sam McIntire visual materials collection, Bentley Historical Library, University of Michigan, (right) Raymond McCoy, *Mackinac Island, Michigan – Showing Main Roads and Trails and Points of Interest;* **120** Thomas Pfeiffelmann, print from Superior View/Jack Deo; **121** (ad) *Mackinac Island News,* July 18, 1942 from the *Mackinac Island News* collection, Bentley Historical Library, University of Michigan, (lower) Archives of Michigan; **122** Illustrated Postal Card Co., N.Y. ; **123** (upper) E.C. Kropp, Milwaukee, Wis., (lower) S.A. Poole-Wickman Photo; **124** (left) *Selected Scenes of Mackinac Island Hand Colored,* circa 1910, (right) V.O. Hammon Pub. Co.; **125** V.O. Hammon Pub. Co.; **126-127** Detroit Publishing Co.; **128** (left) *Mackinac Island News,* July 31, 1943 from the Grand Rapids Public Library, (right) Archives of Michigan; **129** Archives of Michigan; **130** (left, upper & lower) Lake County (IL) Discovery Museum, Curt Teich Postcards Archives, (middle) V.O. Hammon Pub. Co.; **131** (upper left) courtesy of Alan Bennett, (upper right) Clarke Historical Library, Central Michigan University, Pere Marquette Statue Collection, (lower right) *Selected Scenes of Mackinac Island Hand Colored,* circa 1910; **132** G. H. Wickman Publisher; **133** (ad) C.C. Eby, *Mackinac County of the Straits Country,* circa 1924, (postcards) Lake County (IL) Discovery Museum, Curt Teich Postcard Archives; **134** Clarke Historical Library, Central Michigan University; **135** (left) V.O. Hammon Pub. Co., N.Y. (right) Detroit Publishing Co.; **136** (upper) Michigan Central Railroad, *The Fairy Isle of Mackinac,* circa 1890, from the Clarke Historical Library, Central Michigan University, (lower) Clarke Historical Library, Central Michigan University; **137** *Selected Scenes of Mackinac Island Hand Colored,* circa 1910; **138** (left) J. Koehler, N.Y., (right) Nelson & Sons Co., Chicago; **139** (left) Michigan Central Railroad, *Mackinac Island and Michigan Resorts,* 1930, (upper right) John H. Schwegler, Mackinac Island, (lower right) Lake County (IL) Discover Museum, Curt Teich Postcard Archives; **140** Superior View/Jack Deo; **142** Archives of Michigan; **143** (left) V.O. Hammon Pub. Co.; **144** Archives of Michigan; **145** Detroit Publishing Co.

We have credited every image that had a publisher indicated. All unaccredited mages had no notice of publisher. For organizations, we have used the name that was contemporary to the time of the illustration. Arbutus Press will be pleased to rectify any credit omissions or inaccuracies in future printings.

Index

About the Authors

Christine and Tom share a love of northern Michigan and a fascination with its history. They are especially interested in the history of Michigan's tourism industry. Their collection of antique postcards and tourist and travel ephemera was the inspiration for their two previous books: *Vintage Views of Leelanau County* and *Vintage Views of the Charlevoix - Petoskey Region*. Both books have won the Michigan Notable award designated by the Library of Michigan.

Christine Byron is the Local Historical Collections librarian for the Grand Rapids Public Library. She was previously a bookseller for 22 years, working in several bookstores in Grand Rapids and later as district manager for an independent bookstore chain. Christine has an undergraduate degree from Aquinas College and a Master's Degree in Library Science from Western Michigan University. She is an avid reader of Michigan history and has collected old Michigan travel and tourist memorabilia for over seventeen years.

Tom Wilson retired from Sears Roebuck and Company where he held various positions in his thirty-seven year career, including technical manager for Sears Home Serivices. Tom attended Grand Valley State University and is a life-long student of history. He is an avid postcard collector and has collected Michigan real photo postcards for over twelve years. Tom has started a business creating prints from old Michigan and Great Lakes tourist and travel ephemera.

Christine and Tom are active members of the West Michigan Postcard Club. They are also members of several historical societies including the Grand Rapids Historical Society, the Leelanau Historical Historical Society, the Historical Society of Michigan and Friends of Michigan History. Christine and Tom are married and live with their dogs, Max and Willy, in a 1912 Arts and Crafts bungalow in Grand Rapids. They love spending as much time as possible in northern Michigan. This is their third book.